"Heff's Band Aides"
A compilation of techniques presented for the benefit of the aspiring music teacher!

By Eugene Heffelfinger University of Michigan '49 B.M, M.M.

DORRANCE PUBLISHING CO., INC.
PITTSBURGH, PENNSYLVANIA 15222

The contents of this work including, but not limited to, the accuracy of events, people, and places depicted; opinions expressed; permission to use previously published materials included; and any advice given or actions advocated are solely the responsibility of the author, who assumes all liability for said work and indemnifies the publisher against any claims stemming from publication of the work.

All Rights Reserved
Copyright © 2013 by Eugene Heffelfinger University of Michigan '49 B.M, M.M.

No part of this book may be reproduced or transmitted, downloaded, distributed, reverse engineered, or stored in or introduced into any information storage and retrieval system, in any form or by any means, including photocopying and recording, whether electronic or mechanical, now known or hereinafter invented without permission in writing from the publisher.

Dorrance Publishing Co., Inc.
701 Smithfield Street
Pittsburgh, PA 15222
Visit our website at *www.dorrancebookstore.com*

ISBN: 978-1-4349-3757-5
eISBN: 978-1-4349-6858-6

Table of Contents

Dedication v
Acknowledgements vii
Preface ix
Endorsements xi

Chapter One: Overview 1
    Counting 1
    Rhythm 5
    Tone Production-Breath 6
    Tonguing 8
    Double And Triple Tonguing 9
    Articulation 9
    Warm-Up 9
    Dynamics 11
    Tuning 12
    Jaws! 12
    Style 13
    Interpretation 14
    Vibrato 14
    Note Names 15
    Practice 16
    Instrument Care 16
    Alternate Fingerings 17
    Technique 17
    End Of Chapter One…(I Think!) 17

Chapter Two: Woodwinds 19
    Flute 19
    Oboe And Bassoon 20
    Clarinet 22
    Saxophone 23

Chapter Three: Brass 25
   Trumpet, Baritone & Tuba 25
   French Horn 28
   Trombone 31

Chapter Four: Percussion 34

Chapter Five: String Bass 39

Chapter Six: Beginning Band 41

Chapter Seven: Rehearsal Procedure! 44
   Planning 44
   Classroom Management 46
   On With Our Preparations 47
   Instrument Transfer 48
   Festival Preparation 49
   On With The Rehearsal 51
   Chair Position 53
   Older Beginners 53
   Concert Comments 54
   Music Boosters 55
   Class Dismissal 55

Chapter Eight: Marching Band 56

Chapter Nine: More Ensembles 59
   Jazz Band 59
   Pep Band 59
   Pit Band/Orchestra 60
   Solo & Ensemble! 60
   Vocal Music 60

Chapter Ten: Private Instruction! 62

Chapter Eleven: Music Appreciation! 64

Conclusion! 67

Bibliography 69

Appendix A – Risers 71
Appendix B – A-Frame 75
Appendix C – French Horn String Replacement 77
Appendix D – Single Reed Adjustment 79
Appendix E – Snowman 81

Dedication

I want this to be a thank you to all those hundreds of students who accidentally or on purpose entered my classroom since 1949! So much of it seems like just yesterday! The facilities we had to share ranged from a former, dingy, locker room to gymnasium stage (sometimes during gym class), to a cafeteria next to an unfortunate teacher and her fourth grade class! (With thin partitions and an open ceiling!) Later, new facilities included a nice, large room, but with metal and wood shop on the other side of a cinder block wall! (We were informed, "Our music would bother them more than their noise would bother us!") Finally, a completely new high school, which included a fine complex; complete with office, practice and storage rooms and a large library, but even here the wonderful possibility of a useful, upper level was compromised by lowering the ceiling to match that of the adjacent cafeteria; with subsequent "headroom" not convenient for practical use!

Now, because of a millage defeat in Vassar, we escaped to Flint Hamady and another rather limited band room, until an addition to the building included my "dream" facility! I was allowed complete freedom to plan the built-in risers, office, storage, library and practice rooms, and allowed to construct much of it myself! Still, we had to perform concerts and musicals on a gym stage, but this is where we began to do some successful recording, which many of us still enjoy today. Subsequent good fortune, for us (not the taxpayers) enabled us to duplicate these fine facilities at yet another site…and finally, this time, also an auditorium! Hooray!!!

All along the way, I am proud to relate, it was the success my students and I were having, that provided the necessary motivation for administrations to "stretch" their budgets in our behalf!

Now for the main thrust of these remarks, dedication of my book to those faithful students! Not only were they the source of much satisfaction as they grew, in all ways, from 5th thru 12th grades, but what has been even more gratifying, the enjoyment of their transition from dependent "students" to cherished "adults!" Am I wrong, as I travel through these "declining years," to recall with pride the times I now experience personal contact with so many, whether they be from as long ago as the class of '49, or maybe as recent as yesterday's private student? Would that all who read this, sometime also have the opportunity to "cherish moments" of satisfaction like those my students have given me!

Acknowledgements

Hey! I don't want to get all "smarmy" here, but, after all, I do have a conscience, so I want to recognize and thank everyone who encouraged and monitored me in this endeavor…and what a range of "characters" you will find here:

Sister "Louise" (<u>not</u> from a convent), who took one look at the manuscript and said in her usual condescending way, "It <u>might</u> work!"

Retired band director, "Sandy," one who really "knows the territory!" In addition to making valuable suggestions, it became apparent that, from her experienced viewpoint, the idea to compile this information was a good one, exemplified by that comment you always like to hear, "I wish I'd had that when <u>I</u> was teaching!"

Former classmate from long ago, "Meriam," who made such an accurate assessment when she admonished me for some of my many obvious faults! Too many "I's"…stop being humble, apologizing, self-congratulatory… maybe even chauvinistic – but, at the same time, she did give me the encouragement I needed.

Former student from long ago, "Kathleen," a College Professor of Speech no less, who recognized I needed a book on punctuation…(and gave me one!).

Former student from <u>not</u> <u>as</u> <u>long</u> <u>ago</u>, "Chris," pianist and flautist, an aspiring writer of Children's Books, who, while editing some of my grammar, encouraged me to continue my efforts to write in a friendly, enthusiastic style, however daring!

Son, "Bill," formerly enjoying a very successful teaching career as band director at Bad Axe High School, Bad Axe, Michigan, who invited me to work with some of his students, which gave me enough renewed motivation and confidence in my techniques, to carry out my perennial threat to "write a book!"

Daughter, "Sally," a professional musician, I'm very proud to say, (Oboe and English Horn); presently with the Detroit Opera Orchestra and Flint Symphony, who pleasantly surprised me by showing a lot of interest in what "the old man" had to say, and who reminded me of some of the important topics she thought I should include, and finally,

My wife, "Genie" I call her, who has always made me feel that I might just have the knowledge and the ability to "coach" musicians, and who, upon reading my manuscript and discovering the intricacies involved in the teaching of instrumental music, said, "I'm sure glad I played the piano!"

My sincere thanks to all of you!

Preface

Eugene Heffelfinger, B.M., M.M., '49, University of Michigan! That's me! Now age 86, with no real claim to fame, but with quite a few notions about teaching techniques that I have found to be helpful. If you will permit it, I feel capable of providing information that you also can utilize for the edification of your students. I take great pride in seeing my suggestions aid someone in his or her quest to become proficient in musical performance, and it is this same pride that I should expect you to experience if some of my ideas work for you!

I will devote a chapter to overall topics that apply to <u>all</u> students, then, offer suggestions for each of the instruments, followed by rehearsal suggestions for the performing ensembles. I would recommend that you consider reading everything because, even though you may only plan to search for a specific topic, due to deficiencies in organization in a work of this nature, I believe you might find something of value almost anyplace!

I apologize right now for not acknowledging all of the possible sources of information that I will present. This is not to say I am not grateful for everything I have learned from others, but, in the interest of your time and mine, I intend to write as concisely as possible with a flow of words, uninterrupted by considerations of anything but providing helpful hints for you.

Sincerely,

Eugene Heffelfinger

Endorsements

"Lots of good hints and practical advice, most of which could only be found through years of experience! Percussion "stuff" is "spot on!"
Scott Harding, PHD.
Faculty: Music Department, C.M.U.

"The book has a lot of useful information for everyone – new directors, and old ones! Even if one disagrees with some of the material, it serves, at least, to stimulate discussion. I learned a lot and I'm sure others will, too!"
Joseph Dobos, Director of Bands,
East Lapeer HS, Lapeer, MI

"Heff's Band Aides" by Eugene Heffelfinger, might best be titled "Chicken Soup from the heart of a Great Teacher." With a brilliant mixture of wit and wisdom, Mr. Heffelfinger distills his many years of teaching experience into spoonfuls of practical, every day; common sense advice. Teachers of all ages will benefit from the concise commentary of this book and will be readily able to put these teaching tips to good use the day after reading the material covered. Thanks to "Heff" for such a useful collection of ideas!"
Michael Haithcock, Director of Bands and
Instrumental Studies, U. of Michigan

"To tell you that I thoroughly enjoyed every page of your book would be an understatement. You have a humorous, whimsical and unpretentious style that makes for delightful reading. As a young teacher (1953), oh what I would have given for such a book! The practical knowledge you gained by experience and have put in writing would be a godsend for all young instrumental teachers."
Fritz Stansell,
President of Blue Lakes Fine Arts Camp

CHAPTER ONE: OVERVIEW

Where shall I begin? Now that I have promised to give you an overview of hints, I find myself flooded with ideas; so, I will just "dive right in" and begin with:

COUNTING!

For goodness sake, have a <u>system</u>! It is fine to have students imitate your style and rhythm when you are pressed for time and want them to quickly mimic what you would like to hear (especially in <u>jazz</u> band) but, for the most part, a student should be able to count <u>and</u> <u>point</u> anything they are expected to play. This is very essential for accurate performance, which is enhanced if a beat is sub-divided by a foot tap that goes <u>down</u> on the beat and <u>up</u> on the middle of the beat! This beat should be insisted upon from the very beginning because the coordination required will be too difficult to acquire once the notes are more demanding. (Just as a foot-ruler has smaller divisions marked on it for accurate measurement, so does our beat need subdivision if we are to be as exact as professionals demand!)

Let me say more about my suggestion to have students count <u>and</u> <u>point</u>. When they are required to do this, coordination of foot tap, finger-pointing movement and, in addition, uttering the proper syllables, allows the teacher the opportunity to "see inside the student's mind." Be sure the finger taps <u>only</u> on the <u>beat</u> notes and does not tap the subdivisions of the beat. To allow tapping other than the beat would defeat the purpose. Imagine, if students can't do this successfully, how could they possibly simultaneously add still another challenge; that of playing the instrument? And now for an even more valuable reason for doing this counting and pointing: developing the skill of looking ahead! You cannot possibly expect to say the correct syllable at the correct moment if you have not "looked ahead" enough to plan what to say!

Beware of what I call the "spring-foot!" Some students will tap, but their foot "bounces" off the floor, thus missing the middle of the beat, and therefore is rather useless as an accurate subdivision of the beat. We do realize that, while the foot-tap is rather essential during practice, it is highly desirable to avoid having a stage full of "foot tappers" during a concert! Don't let anyone tap his <u>heel</u>! This causes the thigh to jump up and down and is <u>really</u> distracting! I recently witnessed a French horn ensemble member tapping the heel, actually moving the thigh that the horn rested upon!

Hey! Did you know there is a little "rhythm regulator" in the ankle? This is what enables us to walk or march with a steady gait! (When inebriated, it doesn't work too well, causing noticeable "staggering" to occur…no "personal" experience here!)

I do not necessarily appreciate the common system of "1-e-&-a" because all the syllables have a rather imprecise beginning! Although they can be helpful, you will notice the syllables are not as percussive as "1-tee-tay-tuh". The latter method of counting also utilizes a tongue action that closely parallels the action of the tongue in wind playing. I <u>do</u> have to admit that it is much simpler to write "1-e-&-a on a student's music.

You will notice in the following illustration, I have purposely placed each portion of the beat in a vertical alignment. Even so, I seldom find a student capable of the reasoning I would expect as they try to determine which syllable to use, even though it seems so obvious. You usually have to help them see the relationship.

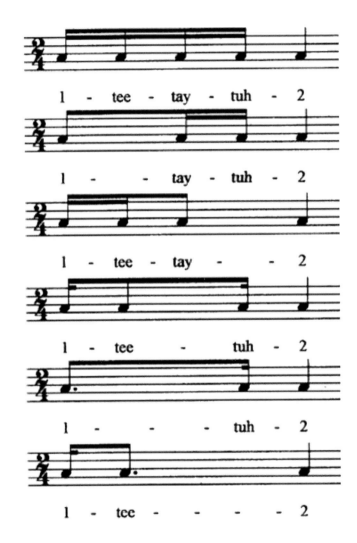

When teaching the meters 6/8, 9/8, etc., I recommend the use of "1-la-le, 2-la-le," etc. as opposed to some of the impractical systems I have observed. One notable example I can recall was to say "Ithica," which is fine for a triplet but provides absolutely no assistance for any subdivisions! Conversely, with the system I favor, subdivision is very adequately covered by the syllables, "<u>1</u>-ta-<u>la</u>-ta-<u>le</u>-ta" etc. When counting, say only those syllables that apply to the rhythm of the notes. Skip the syllables that have no note. It is useless to say un-needed syllables. Hey, don't you be afraid to say these syllables in front of a bunch of teen-agers! At first they will doubtless "snicker," but, if you insist, they will soon get the message, and the benefit!

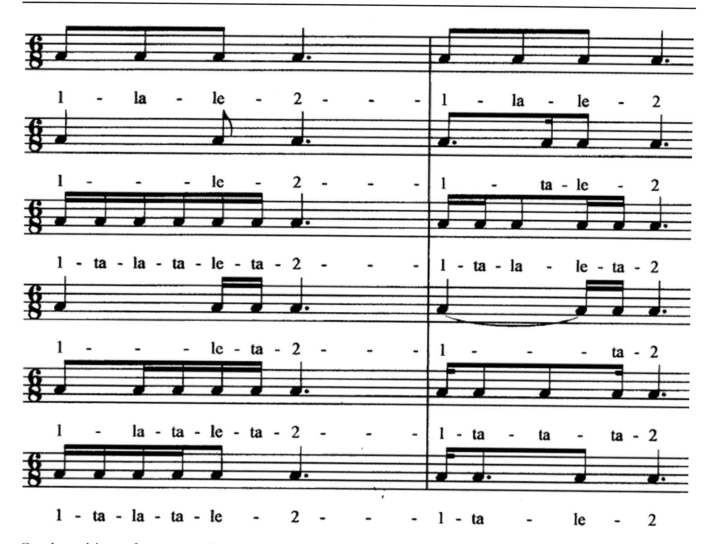

On the subject of compound meter, can't we all admit that this is just a way to write triplets without having to mark them as such? Very efficient if the bulk of the music is based on triplets. So, we actually find ourselves with meters that are simply one, two, three, or four beats of triplets! Who will profit by counting from one to twelve in 12/8? Maybe a tempo marking that is so slow that the conductor feels he should subdivide the beat could logically be counted in 6, 9, or 12, but, I submit that even "Silent Night" has only the feeling of "two" (like the rocking of a cradle). Counted as "1-ta-le-2" is so practical! I would shudder to hear someone count "1-2-an-3-4-5-6!

Let's see if we can put into words the often-noticed problem created when students <u>do not</u> place the proper emphasis on the correct portions of a beat. There is the tendency for students to put stress on the first note of a group of sixteenths <u>no matter</u> on <u>what part</u> of the <u>beat</u> a group begins. When the beat falls on the first sixteenth, no problem. That is where the most stress normally <u>should</u> be placed! But, let's say you first have a sixteenth <u>rest</u>. Then you should not stress the first note, because if you do, you create an awkward rhythmic feel to the phrase. The best way I can describe this is as follows: With a group of four sixteenths, the first note gets the most stress, the second and fourth note get less stress, and the third note gets less than the first but more than the other two. Now, when <u>rests</u> are placed on any of these sixteenths instead of notes, the remaining notes still get the same proportion of stress as before rests were inserted! Often a student's rhythm may seem faulty because of an incorrect placement of stress!

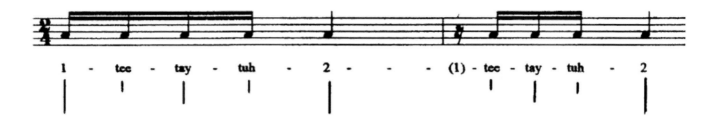

While I think of it, can we clear up the trouble students have with dotted quarters? Poor kids! They learn that 1-1/2 is between 1 and 2 in arithmetic! Then, in music, 1-1/2 beats end <u>between</u> 2 and 3! I compare this to the foot-ruler that starts at <u>zero</u>, and the musical measure that starts at <u>one</u>! Understand?

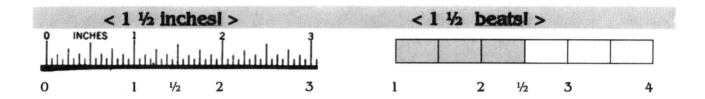

Now would be a good time to bring up the subject of note duration. Again, misunderstanding of arithmetic leads to lack of precision at the <u>release</u> of longer tones. For example, a half note is often cut short because the student doesn't realize that, in music, a half note starting on count <u>one</u> of the measure, must be sustained until count <u>three</u>! I use this method of counting; One-two-OFF! Three-count note; One-two-three-OFF! When an ensemble has notes of this duration, this method of counting assures you of an <u>end</u> to the chord that is just as precise as the <u>beginning</u>!

Perhaps an even better way to explain all of this would be to emphasize that any note <u>ends</u> at the point the next note (or rest) <u>begins</u>!

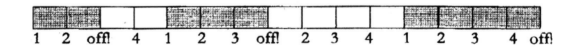

Before we leave this topic of counting systems, I must confess that some students seem to learn all the combinations of rhythmic patterns strictly by imitation. I personally profit more by the ability to analyze the combinations, which I feel makes it possible to understand <u>any</u> rhythm one shall ever confront!

RHYTHM!

Since we have found ourselves immersed in the subject of counting, let's finish with the related topic and concern about rhythm. We have mentioned (1) counting systems, (2) foot-tap, (3) length of tones, and now, (4) rhythmic problems.

The dotted eight followed by a sixteenth comes to mind immediately...as it also does to judges who will think you played it incorrectly <u>even if you haven't</u>! With the aforementioned down-up foot-tap, with the "up" marking the middle of the beat, you should be able to play this figure accurately, avoiding the all too frequent "skipping" pattern so often heard. As a fine way of checking your pattern, consider alternating: <u>dotted eight</u> followed by the <u>sixteenth</u>, with the strict pattern of <u>two eighth</u> notes. If you "waltz" the first beat the second will be uncomfortable to play accurately.

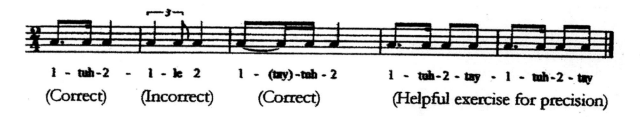

We should also consider "two-beat triplets" which are so prevalent today, especially in jazz band music. For this rhythmic figure I ignore the counting system as such and simply rely on the words, "1-trip-let-3-trip-let." This seems to serve the purpose adequately.

The best musicians in the world use a metronome, not just to establish a tempo, but also to force themselves to adhere to a strict tempo as they practice! So-o-o, why shouldn't beginners do the same! One can be so easily "fooled" by the relation between long and short notes, playing long tones too fast and fast notes too slowly! Actually, a beginner will develop the ability to "listen" while performing with a metronome, all the while developing that precious skill of monitoring what is going on around him even though he is busy negotiating the musical passages! To hear the balance, pitch, tempo, dynamics, etc. of the rest of the ensemble is so essential and it <u>is</u> true, listening to a metronome can instill some of this valuable skill. <u>Insist on this!</u> I once heard a piano student, who was doing a miserable job of adhering to the metronome click, proclaim, "I do my best to ignore it!" I have also heard those who say they 'hate' playing with the metronome, and will not use it, rather than let it be their guide to the benefits mentioned above. (The same can be said about those who won't try to apply a counting system or synchronize a foot-tap!)

Regarding the use of the metronome, during lessons and even with a band rehearsal, I have found it useful, with today's electronics, to amplify the sound of the metronome so no one can doubt my assessment of their precision! Playing at a tempo under full control, then <u>gradually</u> increasing to a faster level, can be a valuable aid for developing technique and can be such a motivation as you challenge yourself to play at speeds that are more impressive! All of which causes me to mention the need to "read around the notes," as one of my college professors was so often to admonish. Expect a student to fully understand the metronome markings as well as words (in whatever language) that give clues to tempi and style. Spend some time helping your student learn to estimate the tempo, using mm=60 as one beat per second, and mm=120, twice as fast (common march tempo). In addition, consider advising students to examine their music to discover the intended "scheme" of the composer regarding dynamics, ritards, a tempo, crescendo, etc.

There are three books I like to use for rhythmic study (as well as technique and flexibility): *Exercises for Ensemble Drill, by Fussell,, 150 Original Exercises by Yaus & Miller, and 101 Rhythmic Rest Patterns* by Yaus. (See bibliography) Each of these books have various attributes which, combined, provide valuable drill.

TONE PRODUCTION!

Most all of the following sections will deal with aspects of tone production, but as an introduction to those areas let me share the observation that, for the mental and physical approach to playing a wind instrument, I think you should consider that, what you do inside your body, determines most of your musical style, tone quality and range!!! Whatever instrument you happen to place in front of you merely acts as the "amplifier" and its shape (and perhaps, the material used in construction…some argument about this!) determines the characteristics that we recognize as flute, trumpet, tuba, etc. This is why I provide so much emphasis on the items that are presented in the next chapters

BREATH!

Now, hang on to your hat! We want to get serious about ALL wind instrument playing. First, take a good breath, (through your mouth and not your nose!) and use it immediately; before you can do something stupid; like locking your throat, thus making a restriction that prevents a strong flow of air. Forget all sorts of comments like "use good breath support," "expand your waist," "don't raise your shoulders," etc. If you simply do, as I will soon elaborate, you will have adequate support, and if you do lock your throat, all the breath support in the world won't help you!

I feel the need to mention more about inhaling properly. Once in a while you will notice a student has made a habit of breathing through the nose…a habit, unfortunately difficult to break! I still visualize my first trumpet lesson (1937) when my band director demonstrated how to keep the embouchure in place while drawing in air through the corners of the mouth. (Caution; there are those who might try to inhale through the instrument!)

In my desire to analyze (at times, not the best teaching method) I like to, rather specifically, describe what is actually taking place at the waist when breath is properly inhaled. The diaphragm, a large muscle in the shape of two inverted "saucers" (one under each lung) is pulled downward, as can be detected by the expanding waist, much like the way an inverted paper plate will spread at the edges if you step on it! Now, and this is extremely important, if the waist doesn't expand the student is getting only a limited use of the lung capacity because the diaphragm has obviously remained in the "up" position. Also, very important, if the student is successfully inhaling; he should not let the waist collapse when exhaling! Instead, allow the relaxation of the rib cage to facilitate the process of exhaling. I look back with a degree of embarrassment as I recall the years when I assumed the diaphragm could "push" the air out like a piston in a cylinder, but I have since become aware of the fact that muscles are only capable of "pulling," (contracting), or relaxing, not pushing! It IS essential that the waist expands upon properly inhaling, but you should also expect that a good intake also includes the rest of the chest. In fact, by filling up everywhere, we then have the wherewithal to relax the entire structure; shoulders and rib cage, etc., to produce a smooth dependable stream of air essential to controlled tone production. To check expansion of the waist, have the student place the fingertips together in front of the "tummy" and notice the movement that takes place upon drawing a proper breath.

If, while conducting a large ensemble, you give a relatively strong preparatory beat, say for the beginning of a stirring march, do you notice the "air being sucked out of the room?" You will probably find a relatively untrained group creates no sound at all! If the proper breath is taken, it will be very noticeable, believe me! Incidentally, it has been my experience that, all according to the personality of the student, he or she may regard it as offensive to make the obvious sound that is made if a full breath is taken very quickly through the mouth. You may have to "sell" the idea that it is only proper and advisable to take a breath in the manner described. (You may have noticed this sound during the breathing by professional TV announcers.) So often students do not sustain tones for their full duration because, if they have the habit of inhaling slowly, they have to cut notes short in order to breathe in time for the next downbeat. Obviously, "quick breath," at the last moment, will solve that problem. Incidentally, the military must have been "on to something" when they required us to have good posture! You will discover, that when the shoulder blades are forcibly drawn toward each other, proper, healthful, useful breath is a by-product! Try it! You'll like it…especially when walking!

You can check student's power by holding a piece of paper about 2-feet away. Then we compare how much disturbance we can create by taking a breath and blowing a healthy stream of air at the edge of the paper! There should be lots of movement, if done with proper breath! (Bernoulli's effect as learned in science class.) You may notice that while leaning back in a chair, as long as you move the small of the back forward, you can take adequate breath that is not possible if you "slump."

In addition to speculating about how to take a breath, I would like to share two other observations regarding breathing. First, I recall a flute quartet that was "getting nowhere" in one of our practice rooms…that is, until I really badgered them about their shallow breathing, and do you know, I am positive the extra attention to breath made them so alert that we proceeded to have much more success, almost as though the breathing did something for their brains!

Second, along the way in this teaching career, I discovered that, if I took gigantic breaths almost to the point of bursting…then held the breath for a few seconds, then finally, exhaled till completely empty of air (almost inside out!) I thereby could induce an amazing feeling of relaxation! (At times, while trying to sleep, two or three of these "cycles," and I am off to dreamland!) I have since become aware of a more detailed method of doing almost the same thing…inhale 4 counts, hold for 7 counts, and then exhale with resistance slowly for 8 counts. (No need to "hurry" the repetitions.) I find this even more effective than the method I first described! It seems that concentration on counting comes close to "counting sheep!" (Incidentally, this also seems to help me when I try to prevent a cold!)

Well, you know I just had to share this information with my band and, much later, discovered that this is somewhat the procedure recommended by several other sources, one of them being "Yoga." Now…a surprise! I subsequently discovered that, simply being a "band director" (sarcasm intended) it was not entirely "legal" for me to dispense such information! How do you like that! You will have to formulate your own opinion as to the advisability of "sharing your medical knowledge!" It is worthwhile to re-emphasize that there are many healthful benefits to be derived from utilizing "deep breathing!" You will find that, in addition to "Yoga" as mentioned above, there are many other programs that incorporate deep breathing exercises as an important part of the procedures they recommend!

TONGUING

The tip of the tongue should be placed at the upper gum line, <u>not</u> behind the lower teeth. The area of the tongue immediately behind the tip of the tongue should be <u>low</u> and <u>flat</u> (bottom of mouth), as opposed to raised against the roof of the mouth! Test yourself! Tongue raised – an "airy, hissing" sound! Tongue flat – a "wholesome, roaring" stream!

Don't neglect this next item that I consider to be one of the most effective remedies for tone and pitch production…namely, the use of the <u>back</u> of the tongue! <u>All</u> wind instrumentalists will profit if they form the pitch in their mouth, much as a whistler would. In fact, I feel that the singing, whistling and wind instrument performance are all related. Don't give me that argument about closing the throat if you raise the back of the tongue! Try this: a low "roar" for the lowest pitch you can make followed by a glissando up to a "hiss!" You may notice a <u>transition</u> <u>point</u> where the tongue seems to shift from depressed to arched. I have found that brass students who have difficulty with range do not make this transition to a hiss. (At about fourth line "D," treble clef.)

Incidentally, I feel that <u>every</u> <u>single</u> <u>note</u> is aided in intonation by having the tongue very carefully placed in the manner suggested. Also, the tone quality is surely enhanced when the pitch in the oral cavity is in sympathetic resonance with the pitch the instrument is expected to produce! So often we find students thinking like a monotone, yet expecting the horn to play all the notes. Often, without really clarifying the issue, teachers will be heard to ask that you must "think the pitch." I consider this an incomplete description of what really needs to take place. Frequently I request that the student remove the horn from the lips, and demonstrate the ability to form the pitch desired with just an air-stream. You would be amazed at how much this request reveals a student's "good ear." Some can display a pitch that is so accurate it could almost be converted into a whistle, right in tune! In fact, you can recommend using that same air stream to "play" songs, something I recall doing during my Junior High days when, with music forever in mind, I did just that until my teacher insisted I stop being "disruptive!"

Let me make it clear that I feel that even the woodwind instruments profit by this careful placement of the back of the tongue. However, with the brass, it is absolutely essential as it also aids in slurring from one partial to another. True, the lips have their obligation in forming pitches but I consider <u>that</u> almost as a <u>by</u>-<u>product</u> of proper tongue arching. (More on this subject later in topics devoted to brass playing.)

I suppose this is as good a place as any to bring up the argument about which syllable or syllables to use when tonguing, including double or triple tonguing. I can recall my F-horn instructor, from the Detroit Symphony, who suggested several vowels to use according to the register needed. He, however, recommended a series of syllables for <u>parts</u> of the range, when, as I propose, we actually need to adjust that back of the tongue for <u>every</u> pitch. (Just like a whistler!) In fact, I challenge you to make a whistling sound (or just blow air through your lips), and I'll bet you <u>can't</u> change the pitch <u>without</u> moving the tongue as prescribed! Now, blow air over the lips, and, while using the back of the tongue, you will find the ensuing sound to be a continuous adjustment of vowels, starting low with "toe," smoothly transitioning through many of the other vowel sounds and arriving at the highest, "tee!"

Another challenge, closely related to that above, is as follows: form a pitch by blowing an air-stream between your lips. Now, without changing pitch (don't fool yourself here by <u>unconsciously</u> changing pitch) run through all the vowels…a-e-i-o-u. Did you notice that you couldn't change the sound one bit, no matter which vowel you pronounced! There you have, in my estimation, positive proof that it is the position of the tongue that contributes to pitch change! The vowel sound changes, subtly, for every pitch you produce, throughout the range of the instrument!

DOUBLE AND TRIPLE TONGUING!

"Kitty, kitty, kitty" enunciated with the very tip of the tongue by the gum line (upper teeth) is a surprisingly effective way to introduce the necessary feeling for double-tonguing. After you have done this on the instrument, producing short, clean, somewhat percussive tones, try turning the syllables around…"ti-ki, ti-ki, ti-ki" which is the way you would use the syllables in actual performance. (I feel I should clarify the syllable "ti"…wouldn't want to imply "tie" but, instead the syllable, "tee," and "ki" should be "kee.") Just trying to make sure there is no misunderstanding!

If you want a good argument, when engaging in a discussion of triple-tonguing, bring up the relative merits of "tu-tu-ku" as opposed to "tu-ku-tu, <u>ku</u>-tu-<u>ku</u>!" Actually, there are times when each method is advantageous. I feel that the double-tonguing is very efficient compared to the "tu-tu-ku" but you have to really be capable of alternating the emphasis from "tu" to "ku" when using the double-tongue pattern on triplets! For example: "tu´-ku-tu, ku´-tu-ku." There are times when this fits the music very well, but there are also times when "tu-tu-ku" is more appropriate. If you are really good at it, who cares which method you use!

ARTICULATION!

Don't you hate it when students ignore attention to tonguing and slurring? Oh, there are a multitude of exercises that give practice for the myriad of combinations possible, but when it comes to <u>using</u> the requests of the composer or arranger, there is not usually enough consistent attention to details. I have found it very helpful to aid the physical and mental coordination required by using the following method: Say "ta" to start each slurred group and "la" for each successive tone under the slur. Thus, for slur two, tongue two, you would say "ta-la-ta-ta" and for tongue one, slur two, tongue one, you would say "ta-ta-la-ta." A long phrase slur ending with a tongued note would become, "ta-la-la-la-ta"! (This is one of those explanations that are much easier to demonstrate than to put in writing…but so worth the effort!) It can become fascinating to go through all the possible combinations of slurring sixteenth note groups while using these two syllables. Try it, and you'll buy it!

WARM-UP!

It has been said, that once a muscle is strained, it can never regain its original quality. This may have been an exaggeration, but why take the chance? A muscle that is cold is not elastic enough to take as much of a shock as a muscle that is "warmed-up." Take a cue from athletes…never would they attempt to compete without adequate warm-up! I picture a muscle that is cold as though it is brittle like a thin sheet of ice! Apply pressure and it disintegrates! Thoroughly warmed up, a muscle can snap back as though it were elastic! Now, how can a student warm up somewhat like the professional who will devote at least half an hour to careful warm-up? Well, when he or she is rushing to class, it will not be possible! The director should provide some time for <u>individual</u> warm-up and then also plan to provide additional time for some <u>organized</u> warm-up. (It would be practical to do a bit of preparatory blowing and even "buzzing" while walking to class, but that is something I would not necessarily recommend with other students nearby! (Ha!)

Since we mentioned the professional and his half-hour warm-up, we may as well expand on that topic just a bit. The key here is to have a very gentle beginning to the process. Blow air between the lips…pause…buzz the lips…pause…then blow air through the mouthpiece…pause…buzz the mouthpiece…pause…blow some very relaxed tones. (As his warm-up I used to hear a fellow in college, blow the strangest, ugly, low tones on his trumpet — now I understand the wisdom of that approach.) Pause…then, finally, do some lip slurs, gradually extending the range. Most of this is especially essential for a brass player, however. Notice the emphasis on pausing frequently…this is highly recommended!

Hey! I just caught myself using the word "buzz!" Allow me to digress a moment to present a theory of mine guaranteed to create excitement in the "intellectual music world!" While "buzzing" a mouthpiece is a rather simple way for a beginner to get a brass instrument to respond, I don't really believe that a musician with good tone quality <u>actually</u> <u>does</u> <u>that</u>! Instead, I believe they just "think" they are doing that, when, in reality, they have gravitated to the air stream I have been recommending, formed when you do the previously mentioned "roar to a hiss!" By way of furthering your consternation, hold your hand in front of a "buzz." Where, tell me, is the strong air stream we always ask for? Huh? Now, simply blow and "roar and hiss!" There's a real stream!

You know? On this question of "buzzing;" just blowing a plain stream of air <u>is</u> a <u>vibration</u>, and, as I raise the tongue from as low as possible to as high as possible (that "roar" to a "hiss" I continue to mention), THAT is what I use to produce tone on the brass instruments! Further, and sort of interesting, and I know not why, but the "range" of those tongue movements is…get this…about two and a half octaves! That is approximately the same practical range on all of the instruments, as well as for my whistling, the usable harmonics on a violin string, and even my singing (if I include falsetto)! Have I discovered something here? Is this, perhaps, also true for you?

Want something else to puzzle about? As I alluded to earlier, I think that, even the woodwinds profit by this tongue position which I will now mention for the "umpteenth" time…even the flute! You don't do any "buzzing" on those instruments, do ya'! No, you blow a stream of air and I don't think you should neglect forming that pitch inside of you to match want you want to hear on that instrument! Here's another item to consider; if you don't have a proper embouchure, you can't move the back of the tongue as desired… can't do it too readily when you "buzz," either!

Back to "warm-up." Each person must develop his or her own procedure! I don't particularly care for long tones at this stage. I feel that such continuous effort in the beginning is too tiring. Even when warming up the voice I don't recommend maintaining the same syllable for long periods. Anytime muscles are in the same active position for an extended time it can cause fatigue. (The heart muscle, you might know, rests <u>between</u> beats!) Do realize, however, that long tones, with crescendo and diminuendo, are very useful for developing endurance and control of dynamics; not to mention the fine opportunity to monitor the tone production, pitch, quality, intonation, etc.

On a personal note…I can't mention careful warm-up without recalling New Year's Day in 1948. Many fellow WW2 veterans, in our University of Michigan Band, rebelled at the idea of marching 5 miles in the Rose Bowl parade because they were anxious to do their best during the half-time show at the big game. (At least that is the reason they gave!) Well, we did have to march after a hotly contested re-vote on the subject! I shall never forget how good I felt after the long parade because the alternate playing and marching for that period of time qualified as the best "warm-up" you could desire! (We "knocked them dead" during our half-time show and the team won 49 – 0!) Let us reiterate - take time for careful warm-up!! Let us not foster the abuse of the delicate muscles involved in performance!!!

DYNAMICS!

One of the essentials of a musical performance is volume change…for my taste, it might occur from moment to moment! In many cases, don't wait even one measure before attempting to add interest by subtle changes in dynamics!

How to do that? Hey, let's add the word "amplitude" to our vocabulary! We borrow this term from the scientists! In physics you will find that anything that vibrates will move from a very limited position for a soft volume, to a more violent position for a loud volume. This can be demonstrated on an oscilloscope which shows what is called a sine wave…the softer the tone, the smaller the deviation from a still, straight line, while the louder tone is pictured with a large deviation from the central position. Now, whether it be your vocal chords, your lips, the reed, the strings, or even your drum sticks, the more you allow the vibrating mechanism to have lots of amplitude, the louder the sound will be! Notice, I mentioned you should allow the mechanism, (lips, reeds, etc.), to vibrate! Do not FORCE! I like to say, "LET it get louder."

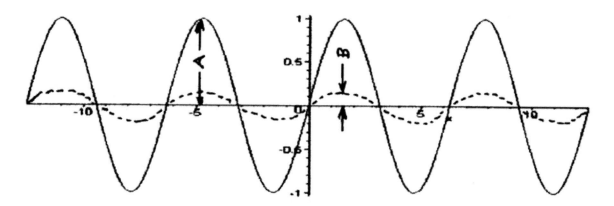

Amplitude at "A" denotes "loud." Amplitude at "B" denotes "soft."
(Pitch is constant as denoted by width of the arcs.)

You will find that you can maintain the pitch if you use this approach, otherwise, the pitch of brass instruments will go sharp as you strive to make a louder sound. There is a "tricky" procedure necessary to really hold the pitch. That is, as you increase volume you must relax a bit to allow for the increased stretching. You probably realize that the more you stretch a string the sharper it gets? Well, this can be observed on a tuner if you take for example, a string bass, and bow a real loud sound…the pitch rises a bit, which you can detect with a very sensitive tuner! While we are at it, the string bass gives you a fine example of amplitude. On a soft tone you will barely be able to see the string move, but on a loud tone it will move as much as an inch!

Now, how to apply this to the woodwinds? Well, how do you like THAT! The reed instruments go flat as you increase volume! What a mess this can make in ensemble playing! Make a crescendo and the brass goes <u>sharp</u> and the reeds go <u>flat</u>! If you have your lips formed properly (somewhat like a drawstring on your pajamas) you will <u>let</u> the little circle of muscles get larger for loud and smaller for soft, allowing the reed or reeds to really "dance around" (amplitude!) for loud, and be somewhat curtailed, in their movement, for soft. It is easier to make a loud sound when you are a beginner, because it doesn't take as much control as playing softly.

So often the reeds will sound "mushy" when they are required to play softly. This is when I emphasize that you must "work hard and only let a little come out!" (So often, students mistakenly assume that you blow "hard" to get loud and "not so hard" to get soft.) If you aren't intense on soft tones, you lose "carrying power" AND tone quality!

On the brass instruments, if you have the proper jaw position and sort of "clench" the lips at each <u>side</u> of the <u>mouthpiece</u>, you will thereby define the limits of the "string" (the lips inside the mouthpiece) and this is the vibrating mechanism that we control, <u>letting</u> it really "flap" for loud or restricting vibration (not pinching) for soft. Remember that word, <u>amplitude</u>! Be sure to emphasize that, while "clenching" the corners, you need to <u>allow</u> that portion of lips in the mouthpiece to be free of undue tension.

TUNING!

In addition to the above information relating to pitch change, there is the necessity for much individual attention to tuning instruments to the band's concert pitch of B-flat. Since this is such a specialized procedure it will be covered in subsequent chapters as the need arises. However, since so many students of brass come to me with tuning slides drawn an excessive amount because of faulty tone production, I find it helpful to use a bit of my "math minor" to explain that adding too much length to the tubing destroys the "proportion" between the relatively fixed lengths of each valve slide. As an example: if to the fraction 2/4, one <u>adds</u> 2 to both numerator and denominator, you now have 4/6 or, reduced by <u>dividing</u> top and bottom by 2 (permissible function) you now have 2/3, a "ruined" proportion. Moral of the story…learn to properly produce tone, as emphasized frequently in this treatise, so it will be unnecessary to draw the tuning slides so excessively!

JAWS!

Say, "AH!" Now, carefully move your lips to an "OOH" position. Well, what do you know! This is a fairly reasonable position for a<u>ll</u> the woodwind instruments! You will notice that, with the jaw in this position, you can make all those movements of the back of the tongue previously mentioned, but if you have your jaw relaxed as it would be if you are idle, you can't begin to form all those pitches we desire inside your mouth! In fact, the way some students hold their jaw makes it even difficult to talk plainly. (Jaw loose with tongue lying flat in the bottom of the mouth!) Try this: Form your embouchure and try to talk. If done correctly you will sound very normal, but if you lower your tongue and round the chin, then try to talk, you will sound ridiculous! This then is a convenient check on students and their jaw formation. How to make them <u>stay</u> in the proper position is another story!

It is also desirable to have what I call a "clenching" of the lips and teeth at the corners of the mouth, almost as though you are trying to bite the lips at each corner of the mouthpiece! Don't be satisfied unless you can adopt this position…and keep it! I'll admit it is very frustrating to see a student hold the jaw in a perfect position…and then lose it when they start to blow!!!

Another hint that may help the concept of embouchure formation would be suggesting that you could imitate the blowing of a balloon. This even has the effect of getting the tongue in a pretty usable position!

A very well known college professor of clarinet once tried to get a student to maintain this jaw position by holding a pencil against the jaw. I didn't find this to work too well. I submit that, if you really want to get to the bottom of this problem you will find it necessary to have the student <u>stop</u> dropping the back of the tongue into a low relaxed position. <u>That</u> is what causes the problem…that lousy, low tongue position! As soon as the back of the tongue is arched, and kept there, the jaw will assume the position we want and need!

As I may mention other places in this treatise, I feel that this may be why setting the embouchure for high notes on brass instruments will enable one to play high <u>and</u> low, however the reverse (setting for low) will not work well for high as the tongue is too low and lets the jaw relax too much.

When we discuss brass playing I will call attention to the necessity to keep the lower lip firmly <u>against</u> the lower teeth. (This also helps avoid the "bulging" upper lip!) I will just mention now in passing, that students who lower their head often are in a position that prevents this necessary firmness against the lower jaw. This I shall review later! (I demonstrate by blowing my best tone for them, and then let them hear what happens when I duck my head the slightest amount!)

STYLE!

If-you-want-to-sound-like-a-ba-by, you-dis-con-nect-each-syl-a-ble! This is the way all too many students play when song style is required! I believe that, early on, the students should be taught to tongue <u>while</u> blowing! This is how to develop a fine legato style. There is plenty time to use marcato and staccato at a later date. Song style is what we want when they play the little ditties that they find in the beginning lesson books. Play like you sing! Play like you talk! The breath is absolutely continuous under these circumstances during the length of a phrase or sentence!

A helpful way to illustrate this might have the student picture a stream of water that you interrupt with a "flick of the finger" rather than to "turn the faucet on and off!"

While I think of it, let me mention that the trombone player <u>has</u> to have this technique when the rest of the class learns to slur. He or she should also be ready to make quick, last moment moves to the new slide position <u>while</u> tonguing and blowing! True, when the slide goes <u>down</u> and the note goes <u>up</u>, and <u>vice versa</u>, you can make a <u>natural</u> <u>slur</u> without tonguing. This is fun to do.

Beware of the habit of "locking" the throat! If you hear any "grunting" it is a symptom of a throat that is restricted — nothing gained by telling <u>these</u> students they need more "breath support!" This is the student I tell about the idea of holding their tongue as though they were cooling off a "hot potato" with their breath! (Probably, there <u>are</u> those who never tried this!)

When the need arises for marcato or staccato style, <u>then</u> we can introduce the notion of <u>letting</u> the notes stop. Notice we said "letting," because we know we must avoid that habit of jamming the tongue forward to make a "tutting" effect. As I understand it, we do not really have a good explanation of what really happens when a tone stops. There is sort of a suspended animation…a moment where we dare not really relax the blowing mechanism. (It must stay ready for the next note.) I like to describe this to students by holding my fingertips of one hand behind the curved fingertips of the other hand to imitate the action of the tongue as it draws back from the teeth, and returns to the teeth only <u>after</u> the tone stops, (rather than being returned to the teeth while still producing tone, which would cause that "tut" we mentioned above). My college days have caused me to be sort of a "nut" about marcato style! Oh, how neat it is to hear notes, held as long as possible, yet with "daylight" between them! When an entire ensemble does this unanimously, the effect is so, well…effective!

INTERPRETATION!

We probably could have called this section, "expression!" If one has nice tone, and all the other important rudiments of playing, there is still usually an amateurish sound to a young student's playing until he or she can really change dynamics, use rubato, and even include vibrato! Simply following instructions like crescendo, diminuendo, ritard, etc., still does not produce what we would consider a musical performance. I like to ask students to become "actors" in order to "feel" or "conjure up" the essential qualities that make music interesting! As with attempts at vibrato, I know that students, at least as young as Middle School age, can be expected to add these ingredients into otherwise proficient performances. Students must be convinced that they have permission to "let their hair down" and emote in order to create an interesting and enjoyable performance. Never do we want to be guilty of "just playing notes!" This would not be sufficient for our musical satisfaction! Be expressive, even at an early age!

In this regard I recall a revered college professor in the Education Department who stressed that students must learn to "read around the notes!" I confess that it took me years to realize that some students could not respond, even to eighth notes or sixteenth notes, because their attention was directed so specifically at the "note-heads" that they didn't even notice the flags! As you might expect, key signatures, meter, dynamics, tempi and articulation will be ignored if we don't emphasize "reading around the notes!"

As a further bit of emphasis in the quest to have young musicians sound mature, I was rather bold in branding a poor performance as "thoughtless!" That was my measuring stick! Was it a "thoughtful" rendition?

VIBRATO!

If you are a singer, it is almost impossible to feel comfortable singing a "straight" tone. (As I understand it, the famous "St. Olaf" Choir <u>did</u> attain some of its reputation in a cappella singing by purposely requiring its members to sing in that manner.) For our purposes, we need to rely on the "natural" desire we have to utilize vibrato, like a singer, and apply this to our various instruments.

If you observe a violinist or cellist, you will see the sometimes almost "violent" movement of the hand on the strings. We can learn from watching this. Performance is enhanced when vibrato is used and we can also see that the "speed" and "amplitude" varies according to the degree of excitement desired. You could also notice that, on an open string where you cannot alter the tone, the "musical" quality of the sound is lacking somewhat.

Now, how to apply vibrato to the wind instruments? Unless you are playing "jazz" don't do it on the clarinet or French horn! (That, at least used to be the tradition, but modern practice does allow for some exceptions.). Other instruments? Well, we have various methods to utilize. "Intensity vibrato" refers to the technique of altering the strength of the air stream using a feeling of "Oo-oo-oo," or "Hoo-oo-oo." On most woodwind and brass instruments we can use a "jaw" movement such as "Woo-woo-woo." Trumpets, all according to the style of music, may make very good use of a "hand" vibrato. And, on the trombone, we can move the slide back and forth in a short, quick motion that very much approximates that of the string player. When using "jaw" movement, (activating the "hinges" at the sides of the jaw), be sure to include plenty of breath support, too. Incidentally, be glad you don't have quite the necessity for the coordination required on violin where you make the hand on the string move back and forth, while the hand on the bow must maintain a smooth, steady stroke in one direction!

In much of this attempt to add interest to our performance, we are rapidly altering the pitch and the volume of the tones and, if done well, we, like the string player, must also alter the "violence" and the speed of the vibrato. Be judicious in the use of vibrato! In days gone by, an exaggerated vibrato was called a "Nanny Goat" vibrato. Once again, if you haven't had "barn yard" experience this comment won't mean much to you!

When beginning the study of vibrato do "exaggerate" the effect at first. Slowly alter the pitch or intensity and let it really have wide latitude to the point of actually being offensive, then gradually "control" the fluctuations to make them musically acceptable. One more point; don't hesitate to have younger soloists try to use vibrato. What a pity to have even high school students play as much as they do without cultivating this very enjoyable aspect of performance!

NOTE NAMES!

Why, oh why, can it possibly be that even high school students, after at least four years of training, can be guilty of not knowing the names of the notes? We know they are the individuals who are forever missing key signatures! Enharmonics are almost impossible to visualize! Alternate fingerings and positions are a mystery!

It is advisable and profitable for every student to be able to draw and label a KEYBOARD! We, who teach, don't seem to realize that, because we can picture the keyboard, it is easy to visualize the relation of notes to each other. Students could have this benefit also, if we provide it!

Thus far I haven't burdened you with many anecdotes, but this one I can't resist! A fifth grade tuba player I was checking for note names, looked at the whole note in the first space, bass clef, and when I asked him to name it he replied, after a bit of hesitation, "O-o-oh?" He did eventually become a fine student but, as you may have guessed, not too many of those kinds of students are around very long!

All of this reminded me; I question aptitude tests! I suppose if all that is desired is a sort of shortcut to a real successful music program; maybe that is a step in the right direction. For my taste, I prefer to try to teach anyone who shows an interest in music. As exhibit "A," I can recall a student, over forty-five years ago, who scored a miserable "45" on an aptitude test, yet, went on to become a terrific trombone player, and is still playing "gigs" today! Man, could he ever improvise! I once had him back as a very impressive guest performer with our Jazz Band! Needless to say, most programs wouldn't even have allowed him to begin!

Eugene Heffelfinger University of Michigan '49 B.M, M.M.

Since I have digressed temporarily, I will also try to make a point by mentioning that, because I was lucky enough to have my daughter's dentist insist that braces would not interfere with her oboe playing, I was able to convince the parents of a very capable sixth grade clarinet player that <u>their</u> dentist, who wanted the child to stop immediately, was, perhaps, overreacting! Braces need not interfere with the correction <u>or</u> the playing! Incidentally, I shared this bit of information with the audience at her graduation concert! She was first chair! (Surprisingly, her mother didn't even recall having had the experience seven years previous!) I understand there is the possibility of using a "dental wax" to cover braces if playing becomes painful but, in my experience, I had no occasion to suggest this but may have been ignorant of possible discomfort of some students. Who knows, I may have lost some students without knowing this was the reason. I <u>do</u> have a feeling that the braces may have caused students to minimize the pressure against the lips, which is not all that bad to contemplate. In any case, I have had many students become perfectly successful in spite of braces.

PRACTICE!

No need to tell you much here that is not obvious, but there are <u>two</u> items I should like to stress. <u>First</u>, to feel encouraged, it seems to be more efficient to work on small sections to a relative state of completion, which gives one a feeling of accomplishment, as opposed to "hacking" one's way from one end to the other! <u>Second</u>, don't be guilty of making a myriad of corrections at once…then saying, "Take it from the top!" Phooey! By the time one gets to the corrections, they will doubtless be no better than before! Rather work on "spots" until they are suitable, <u>then</u> put it all together. Also, avoid spending time on items already perfected to some degree! Even to go back to a few measures you are already capable of playing, is wasted time <u>and</u> effort! Beware of the procedure, however, of merely correcting a note or phrase by simply replaying it! The important requisite here is to <u>successfully</u> go from a <u>correct</u> note to a <u>correct</u> note! Much of the practice is wasted if you adopt the habit of going from <u>correct</u> to <u>incorrect</u> to <u>correct</u>. In this instance, you have not formed the physical and mental progression for successfully negotiating the passage! True, this bit of advice seems like a foregone conclusion, but you must realize, this is so often a faulty practice procedure!

Assuming that successful performance requires attention to so many facets at the same time; notes, rhythms, dynamics, style, tempo, etc., it is only practical for both teacher and student to take steps to simplify passages that are too difficult to navigate immediately. So, be clever enough to make up your own drills with some of the details omitted at first. Often a student will "stumble" when just the counting is requested! How can the rest of the rendition possibly be successful if even the simplified version is a problem! If these suggestions are followed when individuals practice, I think they will be more willing to devote more time and energy to practice because they will <u>feel</u> more successful…and they will be!

INSTRUMENT CARE!

Woe is me! Even adults have a tendency to use their equipment until something fails! Ever heard, "An <u>ounce</u> of prevention is worth a <u>pound</u> of cure?" Well, doing something about it is another matter! Right? Not easy, to be sure, but worth the attention. Clean and oil the bore, grease the corks, oil the pivot points (but not too much), lubricate the valves and slides, etc. More of this later! Oh, oh, I just remembered that students should be cautioned about how they place their instruments when they put them down. Clarinets standing on the bell! Woodwind mouthpieces not protected! Trombone slides not locked! Mallets on the floor waiting to be stepped upon! Brass mouthpiece bouncing around in the case! Cases stuffed with items that press upon keys and slides! Brass mouthpieces dropped, bent, and "tapped" forcefully in the lead pipe! (Ever see one of those "spiral" lead pipes after "daddy" pinched the mouthpiece in a door jam?) Sharp objects on drumheads! And on and on! Someone has to check on these youngsters!

ALTERNATE FINGERINGS!

Every wind instrument that I can think of can be played more efficiently with the sensible utilization of what are called "alternate fingerings!" Perhaps the worst case of neglect is found in the playing of saxophone where students are not taught to avoid those note combinations where you "trade fingers." Rather than learn to use side keys, students are apt to use only the first fingerings they learned. It's a real pity to sacrifice technique for want of a little extra attention to these alternate fingerings, or in the case of trombone, alternate positions. Some mention of this will be found in later chapters, but as an overall observation, we would be remiss if we did not emphasize this aspect of training.

TECHNIQUE!

Think technique, and again I think "*Fussell!*" (See bibliography.) The book is 'tricky' to use in some respects but can be invaluable if used to its fullest extent. One of the shortcomings of a book like this, however, is the lack of material that demands the reading of "rests!" For this purpose consider using "*101 Rest Patterns.*" (Again, check bibliography.)

A real "knack" to be developed is that of "looking ahead!" No one, and I mean no one, is capable of doing anything unless they have at least a fraction of a second advance notice of what they are to do! This technique of looking ahead needs lots of emphasis; not pausing at a bar line, and certainly not at the end of the staff! Be sure to use a tempo slow enough to play the notes and rhythms accurately. So often you will notice someone playing just a bit too fast for his own good; just a bit slower and they are successful! As noted before, any wrong moves are counter-productive...so, slow down! Even the finest musicians who have already mastered a composition must occasionally review their work at a slower tempo or they are apt to get "sloppy!" Doesn't hurt to use the metronome here either, gradually picking up the tempo, as you get more proficient! By the way, how many times have you heard a mistake right near the conclusion of an otherwise fine performance? Aha! Stopped concentrating, didn't ya!'

A serious word regarding performance in public...and, I mean serious! You had better demand high standards of preparation and presentation! There are those who grow accustomed to the many opportunities they have to perform where not too much is expected...not too beneficial for their reputation, or yours! I have witnessed all too many "recitals" where selections were half-memorized, half-read, which is almost always an invitation to disaster! You owe it to yourself to be vigilant in this regard!

END OF CHAPTER ONE...(I think!)

There have been times when, with a feeling of pride, I proclaim that music is the best-taught subject in the school! So nice and practical to have students actually utilize what they have learned; in many cases, with stringent standards of performance plus lots of entertainment value! This, as opposed to the many other fields of learning that come to fruition, if at all, so much later in life!

Then again, when I notice directors continually singing rhythms to be imitated; allowing students to continue...not even knowing the names of all their notes; not providing enough information for students to produce beautiful, enjoyable tone; presenting concerts of limited merit; not developing archives of memorable recordings, pictures, programs and news clippings, for the school and for the students; not instilling appreciation for music beyond the relatively small repertoire of band literature; and, a pet peeve of mine, not encouraging a healthy respect for vocal music; then I am motivated to revise my assessment of our efforts! Maybe, just maybe, that is one of the reasons for my attempt to write this book!

"Ya' don't know what ya' don't know!"

Heffelfinger

CHAPTER TWO: WOODWINDS!

FLUTE!

Well, first off, I will not work with a flute until I check the head joint! If that groove in the cleaning rod is not directly in the center of the aperture, forget it! I have checked entire flute sections and felt lucky to find a single instance where it is as it should be! When the cap comes loose, students turn it tighter and tighter, all the while pulling the plug out of position! The instrument cannot be played in tune with itself under those circumstances. There are times when the plug has become too tight, and times when it is too loose! Also, sometimes the screw on the cap is too loose in which case I add just a bit of substance, paper or foil to the screw. Upper octave too flat? Push plug in a bit. Too sharp? Tune by doing the opposite.

I next want to check the amount of lip covering the aperture. Oh my, you get such a pretty, sweet sound if you cover too much more than a third…but it is FLAT! The octaves also suffer! Not enough covered and it will be sharp and probably "windy!" With the jaw in position, I like the idea of taking a big breath and immediately using it while pronouncing "Pooh". It is nice to see if, while blowing on just the head joint, you can get both high <u>and</u> low pitches, both with the hand covering the end of the joint, and with it removed. Aim that neat little air stream right at the far side of the aperture!

It is not my purpose here to give complete lessons on these instruments! I just want to suggest critical points that I have noticed to be often overlooked. For example, that right hand thumb! Gee, you can't keep those fingers in a good position if you have that thumb way past the bottom of the flute. It's nice to have the flute rest on the fingertip instead and I even prefer having the thumb on the back of the instrument a bit, thereby giving me a bit more stability. (And I like to "push" a little!)

You may be surprised to discover that, by angling the body slightly to the right, with the head straight forward, you can eliminate any "twisting" and tension of the abdominal muscles…and, do hold that flute up!

At the risk of repeating myself, I shall once again refer to my desire to utilize proper tongue and jaw position, "roaring" for low and "hissing" for high, which, incidentally, thrusts the jaw back and forth; also, up and down a bit. <u>Do</u> expect to profit by forming each pitch inside the mouth very carefully.

<u>I sometimes wonder if those teachers who emphasize that you need to "think" the pitch before you play it, were not indirectly having you form the tongue position I am stressing so much!</u>

Many great performers seem to be "naturally endowed" with their skills, but to teach effectively, we can't just rely on those who succeed somewhat "by accident!" We must analyze things enough to be able to help those who aren't so fortunate!

As you may have guessed, I don't want to wait too long before I encourage a student to use vibrato! Golly, I don't want to hear a straight tone any more than I want to hear an open string on a fiddle! "Hoo-oo-oo-oo" with good breath, exaggerated at first, then refined would be a good enough approach! Actually, we refer to this as an intensity vibrato as opposed to a "who-woo-woo" jaw and lip motion commonly used by brass players. A real mature approach to using vibrato includes changing the speed and intensity to suit the emotions of the music and is such a beneficial contribution to expressive performance.

Do clean and lubricate that head and foot joint <u>before</u> you mess up the keys and pads by using too much pressure…and learn how to properly oil those pivot points and check post screws! Don't lose them because of lack of maintenance. (Stay away from pad adjustment screws, however, unless you know what you are doing!)

Hey, don't ignore the B-flat key! Sure, you will have kids who will forget that they can't get B-natural that way, but with all the flats we use in band, it's a shame to saddle the students with "one and one" fingering for the rest of their careers! Speaking of the "B-flat"! a nice drill for positioning the embouchure involves playing the same high B-flat as a harmonic of the E-flat fingering. If you can get the same pitch with <u>both</u> fingerings—and I just loved to alternate them rapidly—you undoubtedly have adopted a fine position for tone production. If the pitch isn't the same, you must alter the amount you cover the aperture.

Along with this exercise let me recommend that you try to play <u>all</u> the harmonics, starting at the bottom of the instrument, playing as much of the harmonic series as possible, "up" and "down!" Harmonics are great for pitch <u>and</u> embouchure!

Now, when you tune your flute, knowing full well that the end-plug is as described at the beginning of this section, play the low B-flat in tune first, assuming you are covering the correct amount of aperture, then play the upper octave to match the pitch. This forces you to use proper tone production. So often those who tune to the high octave first, have an almost useless low register! (Extremely flat!)

OBOE AND BASSOON!

Now you <u>have</u> to get <u>sidewise</u> pressure from your "pucker" or you will ruin every one of those expensive reeds in no time! All woodwinds, with possible exception of flute will profit by the above mentioned jaw position…but double reeds <u>must</u> have it! How often you see the double reed person squeezing on the sides of the reed with their fingers. Hoorah! The reed will stay open for a little while, and then they have to squeeze it again! To enable the reed to have the right contour, you need that sidewise pressure, which, we must admit, is not a common use of our facial muscles, not even on a soda straw! (Although that comes close!) As I write this, I am tempted to suggest flattening the tongue in the bottom of the mouth, just behind its tip (which is at the end of the reed, <u>not</u> behind the lower teeth). With the oboe at my disposal just now, the two reeds I have used for experimental purposes make me feel that this procedure could be every bit as effective on oboe, as it is on the brass!

Now, hand position is important if you are to avoid uncovering those "devilish" holes. I like the example of the "puppy dog" sitting on its hind legs. (My clarinet teacher had an actual picture of one in his studio!) The way the paws droop is somewhat like that which we require. And that right thumb on the oboe! Sure the horn is sort of heavy, and sure it hurts a bit until you are accustomed to it, but, if you are ever to have the fingers where you need them, you must be willing to suffer a bit at first. Don't give in and slide that thumb too far under the thumb rest!

Be sure to moisten reeds thoroughly (preferably with tap water, because "saliva" causes reeds to deteriorate much sooner) before you "crow" on them. Did I say, "crow?" Yes, I did! I don't know why so many people play reed instruments and never check the sound they get while crowing <u>without</u> having the reed on the instrument! It can be so revealing if you observe the kind of results you get by testing in this manner! A good reed, properly "crowed" will make a vigorous, rather violent sound – somewhat like the crow of a pheasant! (Useful comment only for those who have heard a pheasant crow!) The best reed will have a strong "high" pitch with a relatively weaker "low" pitch. Gracious, when you hear that <u>single</u> high pitch some make, you <u>know</u> it is high time to check the embouchure (or the reed)! Oh, that ugly up and down pressure that causes so many problems for an oboist!

My clever teacher didn't call me "Half-hole-finger" for nothing! In one of those "Applied Music" classes required in college, I was lucky enough to readily learn the technique required for the left index finger, pivoting from open to closed <u>without</u> <u>lifting</u> <u>the</u> <u>finger</u>! Unless a student stops lifting the finger from closed to open, of course, they will get notes they do not intend, especially when slurring! This, with the inclusion of "buckle the knuckle" when you add the register key with the left thumb, can be quite demanding but, oh, so important!

You can avoid bent bridge keys if you hold the left hand keys down when assembling the instrument. You know, I seem to be thinking mainly of oboe during this section, but, when I think of the bassoon, a lot of these items apply as well. (Except for those <u>very</u> busy left and right hand thumbs with the overabundance of keys you will find on the bassoon!)

To avoid having the oboe do more harm than good for your ensemble, in addition to having a controlled tone, the student <u>must</u> <u>release</u> the tones carefully or risk sounding like a crying baby! How to do this? Hey, don't move a muscle till the tone stops! Maintain what we like to call the "facial mask!" (Like the Halloween mask that does not move in front of your face!)

Now, please forgive us but we <u>had</u> to get to this point sooner or later…if you want to be good you <u>must</u> learn to <u>make</u> and <u>adjust</u> your own reeds! It just so happens that, when a reed is made, it changes characteristics after it is first completed. Therefore, the maker must return at a later session to further regulate the reed…something not usually done by a manufacturer. For this reason it is not too probable that you can purchase a reed that is just what you need for optimal performance. Also, conditions of humidity, temperature and even altitude can have an effect on your reeds. You need lots of equipment and lots of practice to make good reeds, but <u>it</u> <u>is</u> <u>worth</u> <u>the</u> <u>effort</u>! Here again, it is so advisable to "crow" on that reed! You will get so you can recognize a good healthy crow as opposed to the feeble sound of a reed that is not suitable. Good luck!

When tuning the instrument, it is so desirable to have the reed made and adjusted in such manner that the reed is in tune when <u>completely</u> in <u>place</u>. A little space between the end of the reed and the socket can be problematic. Also, the instrument should be carefully cleaned, including the little register tube!

CLARINET!

Well, let me see your reed! Is it warped? Ah, ha! You are one of those who "gums" up and down thus bending the reed. If you only knew the trouble a mouthpiece manufacturer goes through to get those real critical measurements so necessary for a high quality mouthpiece, you would respect the fact that, when you "warp" a reed, you destroy most of those important specifications! As a personal note, I will admit that, when I discovered a bent reed, I would snap it in two, much to the dismay of the struggling student! So much for disobeying the mandate for a proper jaw position with the requisite "drawstring" embouchure! What with reed prices today, and, ambitious lawyers, I now hesitate to do this!

By the way, that ligature position? So often a student positions it short of the mouthpiece line! Convince them that a short board (the reed) is much harder to bend (vibrate) that a longer one! This brings to mind the question of reed strength. Realize there is a range of care in selecting a reed that goes from little concern about strength and quality, to the extreme of checking an entire box, only to find one or two that are suitable! Some consideration must be given to the characteristics of the mouthpiece, but for the most part, 2-1/2 or 3 reed strength will be satisfactory. Actually, most students gravitate to a strength that suits them and the instructor will be able to monitor the results and make some recommendations according to the sound and response. Be sure to place the tip of the reed just short of the mouthpiece tip. (Interesting to note, at a recent performance by the famous saxophonist, Branford Marsalis, we discovered that he uses reed strength of 5, softened somewhat by scraping!)

Serious students may want to "condition" their reeds by a process of positioning the _flat_ surface on a sheet of glass and then stroking the _carved_ surface in an effort to "seal" the reed. For very thorough instructions, I would like to recommend those of Dr. Ruth Rhodes, a member of the Vandercook faculty in Chicago. (See appendix "D")

Again, by placing the mouthpiece in the student's mouth (sans instrument) a teacher can feel if the teeth are on the top of the mouthpiece where they belong! If you have the student "crow" you can determine if they get a high "c." They didn't? Well, time to get after that jaw position and also require considerable effort from that circle of muscles! Always, after succeeding with a reasonable crow, request that the tongue be used repeatedly to see if the tone can be maintained and to caution against use of any tightness in the tongue, which in turn, tightens the embouchure unnecessarily, in addition to being detrimental to flexibility. (While you are holding the mouthpiece, you can also determine if the right amount of mouthpiece is in the mouth…so often it is too close to the tip!)

When assembling the clarinet, remember that bridge key! Hold down _keys_ of the upper portion of instrument and the big _pads_ on the bottom of the instrument…also grease corks so horn assembles easily. While playing, "wiggle" (rapid alternating) the fingers, slurring to the adjacent keys to facilitate finger position and strengthening. Make sure that students simply add keys without lifting the ones already down! (Do they think they are playing a piano?) Again, we have to check the right thumb and the "puppy dog paws" to assure access to all the keys that are to be played by both little fingers.

When using the register key, "buckle the knuckle," and when trying the relatively difficult maneuver of crossing the "break," "fool" yourself into locating the keys quickly by first playing the note with all the keys pressed, then go to the new fingering ("A" or B-flat) and quickly return to the fingering previously had before your muscles forget where they were! (Don't necessarily let the students know how difficult this may be or you will "psych" them out!) Roll left index finger and wrist slightly for "A"…don't lift finger off the key. Attempt all of this emphasis on crossing the break only _after_ thorough work and success with playing low fingerings with firm tone, followed by quickly pressing the register key, without any change of embouchure, to attain a beautiful, light tone in the upper register.

One of my former students, taught by John Moeller, then at the U. of Michigan, relayed one of his suggestions to me, and I liked it! It was special and enjoyable. Try this: with low "g" lay your reed loosely on the "flabby" tongue thus producing a very "sick" sound! Then gradually draw the tongue backward until the tone clears up! Right at that point you have a tongue position that will enable you to play at a fabulous tempo. Just let your hand "float" up and down the scale, a very satisfying accomplishment…usually dazzling the students! Thank you, Vickie and John!

So often you will hear an entire clarinet section sound "mushy" when asked to play softer dynamics. They are usually guilty of relaxing both embouchure and breath pressure. To offset this distasteful problem of poor tone quality, try to convince everyone that they must work really hard and "only let a little come out!" When you demonstrate this idea, students may think it silly to go to such lengths to make a soft tone, but the lovely intense sound produced in this manner should provide conclusive proof of the necessity for this approach!

Tuning a clarinet should involve more than simply playing c". If you simply adjust the barrel, you have not done enough to check f', or c"', or g"! Frequently you will have to make the "throat tones" <u>flat</u> to get concert B-flat in tune. Let's face it; the whole process is one big compromise! First try f' and c"' by tuning with the barrel. Next, check f" and use the middle joint. Finally, check c"' and, if necessary adjust the bell joint. The high clarinet tones are influenced nicely with this method of tuning. The extra time taken with this process is well worth it but it would be desirable if the student could pretty well learn the amount of adjustment so that, by "eye", the necessary settings can be made without the entire process being required at every session!

When working with the bass clarinet, it is not advisable to have such a firm lower lip. (Should be more like a sax embouchure.) Again, hold the mouthpiece in position and have them crow with a relatively loose lip. Also – put enough of the mouthpiece <u>in</u> the mouth (many try to play with just the tip). REMEMBER THIS…if the student gets the healthy crow we want to hear, it will "<u>jar</u>" their entire head in such a manner that they will probably not want to do it again! Done properly on the instrument you get a big, fat tone and you don't mind the vibration on mouthpiece alone. I firmly believe that one of the reasons for such "puny" tones on a bass clarinet, is that the student <u>prevents</u> this healthy vibration from occurring, much as a "self-preservation" effort, therefore is denied the opportunity of creating a big, rich sound. At times, students <u>immediately</u> switch from "lousy" to "excellent" by simply following this procedure! I am surprised at how seldom students are asked to "crow" on their mouthpieces. It is usually such an unaccustomed request that they are embarrassed at first! Crowing as recommended can be very revealing!

SAXOPHONE!

Here we go with that request to "crow" again! Here it is even more essential than with the bass clarinet! Once you check the mouthpiece on the teeth, and that it is in far enough, and that the ligature is by the line, and that the reed is not bent, and that the tongue is not too tight, a healthy crow will once again "startle" the student! We mean it! The vibration, if done properly, really shakes the entire head!

You will find that many students use a firm "clarinet" style embouchure that makes the tone rather secure, but it is a "rigid" tone. Oh, it will sound fairly decent, but with the saxophone being such an out-of-tune monster, the inflexibility of the pitch is quite undesirable. A clever method of describing the feeling of a correct sax embouchure is to act as though you have an "egg" in your mouth with equal pressure all around – and not too much – or your mouth will be full of raw egg and shells! Understand, however, the relatively loose embouchure we are espousing gives you the feeling of "walking a tightrope!" One wrong move and it is disaster, but how thrilling if done successfully. You will have terrific dynamic capability…from out of nowhere to ponderous and back again! You will be able to influence the pitch all you want which also gives you the potential for luscious vibrato! In short, <u>with</u> this embouchure you are a valuable ensemble member…<u>without</u> it you are a nuisance!

For goodness sake, adjust the strap so the sax fits your <u>body</u>, not vice versa! How hideous it looks to see a "slumped" body with a "twisted" neck on a performer! To relieve hand tension, it is perhaps preferred to hold the alto sax in <u>front</u> rather than at the side but this often prevents the student from keeping a desirable angle between mouth and mouthpiece. In addition, while seated, the front position limits access to side keys! I much prefer the sax at the side for these reasons.

In tuning the sax, once again if time permits, use the short part of the instrument. E-flat concert is recommended. With band, you will use concert B-flat, of course.

Before we leave woodwind discussion, let's reemphasize the need for maintenance! Those pivot points at the posts will rust if not lubricated. Don't overdo this…just touch a needle to the oil supply then to the pivot point. In this way, just the right amount of oil will flow where it belongs. Also, many a horn has been damaged just because the corks have not been cleaned and greased! And…boy, oh boy, don't ignore the endpin screws or they may fall out! Stay away from adjustment screws, however, but let me repeat! Do occasionally see if those screws by the posts are secure!

CHAPTER THREE: BRASS!

TRUMPET, BARITONE & TUBA!

Okay! Let's hear you make believe you are blowing the horn, <u>without</u> <u>the</u> <u>instrument</u>; just the mouthpiece! As stated in the section on woodwinds, the student is usually dumbfounded by the request! Come on! Let's hear it! Well, the usual sound can easily be described, but it would not be polite to do it here! There are buzzes, and then again there are BUZZES! Usually, the "flabby-lipped" buzz you get, sounds just about like that on the horn, especially the low brass! A certain amount of buzzing can be the easiest way to begin a tone for the beginner…if you can call it a tone! Regarding the "buzz", a technique prescribed over and over by teachers of brass; consider this. (You know how much we rely on a strong stream of air!) Well, if you put your hand in front of a "buzz," I think you will be surprised to discover there is lots of saliva, but little, if any, air stream!!!

Now, getting back to forming the embouchure <u>without</u> the horn! We don't even want the buzz at all! Ask the student to "gliss" from low to high with just air coming out, short of whistling, back of the tongue moving up and down, creating what I call a low "roar" up to a high "hiss." We previously mentioned a transition point, about fourth line "D," treble clef, for the trumpet. A student's range seems to be limited until they successfully navigate this transition to an arched tongue, unless, of course, they use excessive pressure and pinching! (Have often noticed that, if I place my fingers under the jaw of a "struggling" student, I can detect a terribly strong <u>downward</u> pressure of the tongue that is obviously not being used properly.)

Holding the lips in such manner that the "red" portion of the lip is rolled inward so the mouthpiece is seated on the "white" upper and lower portion of the lips will be found to be beneficial. It is possible to have the red part of the lips rolled out too far which is not conducive to facility and range. Even a small amount of discrepancy in this regard will have a negative impact! Also, the tip of the tongue should be aimed at the intersection of upper teeth and gum to facilitate "clean" tonguing. We had better not see movement in that lower jaw (except possibly for vibrato). Special attention should be given to these items just mentioned because there are so many <u>less</u> desirable positions possible. While you could play fairly well without obeying these recommendations, for best results these happen to be more imperative than one might suppose.

Right now we want to mention that, if you set your embouchure for a "high" pitch, you will be able to easily play acceptably both "high" and "low," but, if you set your embouchure for a "low" pitch, it will not comfortably be ready to play a "high" pitch. <u>Read</u> <u>that</u> <u>again</u> <u>and</u> <u>never</u> <u>forget</u> <u>it</u>! This is information I first discovered in a book, *Brass Playing*, by Fay Hanson. Wow, all of <u>you</u> may have known this, but I didn't! It works like a charm, and I just wish I had known this about seventy-three years ago!

I imagine most serious musicians do a considerable amount of experimenting where embouchure is concerned. I can recall my first lesson (from First Cornet of the famous Allentown Band, at this writing celebrating its 183rd Anniversary). A lesson, during which, I was instructed to make believe I was "spitting" a seed off the tip of my tongue. I do think this caused me to use a "smile" embouchure that limited me somewhat. Then at college a "pucker" was recommended. This caused me to feel that my first teacher had misled me, but now I think the "pucker" method caused me to let the mouthpiece rest too much on the red portions of the lips contrary to what we recommended in the previous paragraph. Now, guess what? I am back to thinking that my first teacher had the right idea all along, except that I should have refrained from the excessive "stretching!"

I mention this personal information to give you more insight regarding the formation of a brass player's embouchure. As with changing mouthpieces, changing embouchures should be done very carefully because a different set of muscles need to be developed and it will be necessary to be patient to avoid possible strain.

I am reminded that, for some reason I certainly can't explain, the playing of "pedal tones" seems to have great influence on development of a strong and proper embouchure, as well as tone quality, endurance, and, surprisingly, the upper register! (Be sure to maintain proper lip and jaw position as you strive for these extra low tones.)*

When a student has a "pinched" tone, have them play first space "F" and then "wiggle" their horn away from their face. This lets them learn how to "cushion" the lips so that they are held in a manner conducive to fine tone quality. They learn quickly to make the cushion we referred to because if they don't do it, the wiggling would not be tolerable, as it would unduly bump their lips against the teeth! I recall, with considerable satisfaction, that, while judging a trumpet student at a festival, I used this technique to try to improve his very poor tone quality. Immediately, the tone he produced was so pure, the audience applauded!

I often find it helpful to emphasize that there should be a sort of "clenching" of the lips and teeth at the edges of the mouthpiece. This is especially useful for those who have too much tension all across the lips, thus preventing the freely vibrating mechanism that could play all dynamic levels with a ready response to tonguing!

Over and over we find it necessary to tell brass players to hold their head in such a manner that it is possible to keep that "flat" lower lip stretched against the teeth and firmly against the lower jaw. I like to demonstrate what happens to my tone the moment I duck my head while playing…the tone disintegrates immediately!! All according to the structure of the teeth, the head may need to be tilted back rather than lower the instrument excessively.

Speaking of position, have that right thumb between the first and second valve casings. Don't allow that ugly clenching effect you get when the thumb is allowed to slide behind the first valve. This places the fingers in an awkward position. Hold the instrument so you look like an artist! Very little

---

* Could it be that the playing of "pedal tones" conditions the lips to really respond to the extremely complex vibration of harmonics? (Much like that which takes place on a violin string?)

pulling with the little finger, right hand, on the hook that some artists have purposely removed from the instrument. (We recommend you don't even use it except when turning pages.)

After valves have gone up and down millions of times, even after being properly cleaned and oiled, there is a residue that collects at the bottom extremity of the valve's movement. All the oil in the world will not help until this residue is removed by taking off the bottom caps and, when I am in a hurry, I insert the valve from the bottom and gently ream that residue. I would much rather this be cleaned in a more acceptable manner, but at least, when you insert the valve, you notice right away if that is the cause of the poor function of the valve.

Keep all slides clean and greased so they will never be forced so violently that damage is done to solder joints. (Beware of the clown who gets valves and slides in the wrong places!)

I really like to do a lot of lip slurring! At the risk of becoming obnoxious, let me mention once again the movement of the tongue! All you do is tick off the partials (the "harmonic series" that should be familiar to all brass students) from low to high and back again by concentrating on that tongue action. I sincerely feel that the adjustment of the lips is of secondary importance and will be activated properly as a result of the tongue action!

This is as good a place as any to mention that the practice of lip slurring (A misnomer if ever there was one!), lip trilling, double and triple tonguing and "shakes," and vibrato are all good things to attempt because to be successful at any of these, you are almost _forced_ to produce tone properly. In other words, as you attempt these functions, you seemingly arrive at habits that improve what you can do in simple tone production.

Almost every brass student I hear is _not_ capable of a beautiful, singing, legato style. Instead, the breath is interrupted or the tongue closes against the teeth, resulting in an ugly "tut!" So, from a very beginning stage I emphasize _blowing while tonguing_! This is the style that makes those little songs in the beginning of the book sound legato; much like they would be when sung.

Incidentally, I find that, students are fascinated by learning that their chromatic fingerings are based on the fact that the middle valve lowers the tone a half step; the first valve a full step; and the third valve a step and a half! Wow, so that is why you can descend by half steps from an open tone by 0, 2, 1, 1-2, 2-3, 1-3, and finally, 1-2-3! By the way, no instrument can be made completely in tune! Some of those slide lengths are merely a compromise to perfection! Notably, the 2nd valve slide is a bit too long so B-natural will be a bit flat if you don't "lip" it up! Likewise, 1-3, and 1-2-3 will be too sharp unless you lip it down or are smart enough to use the slides, found on more expensive models, that are to be used, trombone style, to favorably alter the pitch.

Tuning of all the instruments can be inaccurate if a student "favors" the pitch rather than play the tuning note with no attempt to influence it. For this reason it is often suggested that the brass player play "sol-la-ti-do", ending on the tuning note. This can be helpful as, in this case, the tone is apt to be normally produced, and not "favored" as cautioned above. Also, the tuning should be done at "mf" so that any distortion due to dynamics can be avoided. In addition, baritones and tubas, if designed with a fourth valve, are better able to control some of the unfavorable pitches one is faced with on a three-valve instrument.

I would suggest that a student should learn all they can about the "harmonic series." This is the group of tones that are formed when you play all of the notes possible with one length of tubing. Two very good reasons for this request: One, a thorough knowledge of the tones helps one understand the many possibilities of "alternate fingerings," and, two, the necessity of playing "in tune" is facilitated by knowing just which pitches in the series are faulty…some flat and some sharp. Following is a description of the series on "open" trumpet. The same relationship applies to all lengths of tubing.

    1st partial - c (also called the "fundamental")
    2nd partial - c' (also called the 1st overtone)
    3rd partial - g' (noticeably sharp)
    4th partial - c" (2nd octave…usually in tune)
    5th partial - e" (probably flat)
    6th partial - g" (sharp)
    7th partial - b-flat " (very flat…unusable)
    8th partial - c'" (3 octaves higher than 1st partial)

Baritone and tuba will need to be carefully held in order to satisfy the need for the jaw position mentioned above. In addition, it is advisable to place the mouthpiece high on the lips…the theory being that the upper lip should have a bigger surface vibrating in the mouthpiece than the lower. According to facial structure, some performers practically touch the nose with the mouthpiece!

Speaking of mouthpieces…if you are a real serious "fuss-budget," you might join the ranks of those who are constantly looking for the "magic solution" for range and tone problems! Me…I shall confess…I don't think I was ever good enough to be overly concerned…just used whatever came with the instrument (usually, "Bach 7C") and was content with the results obtained by utilizing the approach I have been recommending in this treatise! If this causes you to lose respect for my ability, so be it! I have had fairly decent results in over sixty years of teaching, but I realize that, at the level of professional musicians, where the optimum amount of skill is required, it will be practical to investigate every aspect of equipment for optimum performance! (I <u>did</u> like my clarinet students to use the HS* mouthpiece, which were <u>never</u> too inexpensive, but I now note that they cost almost as much as the <u>entire</u> <u>instrument</u> did during my teaching days!)

Some, who switch mouthpieces, might feel playing improves, but upon subsequent sessions, might notice that they are not satisfied as much as they originally thought. Care must be taken when switching from one mouthpiece to another because some very delicate muscles are involved and may be strained if the student expects to adjust too quickly from one to another. For some reason, some people seem to have little problem switching, while others are really disturbed with the slightest change! In a way, using new muscles is almost like beginning all over in their development…the reason you can cause strain if not careful. In any event, switching generally seems to involve compromise of one sort or another. For example, a mouthpiece that allows bigger tone, limits range whereas a mouthpiece ("cheater") that promotes higher range, sacrifices tone!

FRENCH HORN!

First, we wish there would be a way to melt down all the single horns and make them into a monument to the guy who invented the double horn! I have such pity for the families who buy single horns! What ever shall they do with those instruments when they finally are outgrown which, for me would be about two minutes into the first lesson! Please, don't pass them on to anyone in MY neighborhood!

Admittedly, a double horn does cost more and I'm sorry about that, but meet a parent who later finds that the single horn is to be replaced and you begin to realize that "penny wise is pound foolish!"

Don't misunderstand me, a single horn is fine at first and can be played very well but a double horn has <u>many</u> advantages to offer! Even band directors with loads of experience are sometimes lacking sufficient knowledge of the practical and efficient use of the double horn. For being guilty of <u>not</u> learning a tiny bit extra about the double horn, they sacrifice considerably!

Let's explore the advantages: The partials from c' on the single horn <u>are</u> <u>the</u> <u>same</u> as the <u>upper</u> <u>octave</u> on the trumpet. Then, the second octave on the horn is like the <u>third</u> octave on the trumpet! So many open tones! (You <u>could</u> use the first valve to play d", however.) For the single horn then, that means that from c", d" and e" you have only your lip, tongue and ear to depend upon. Yup! No valves! Good luck! With the double horn, you simply push the thumb key (B-flat horn is engaged) and the fingerings become 0, 1-2, and 2! Think you can remember that! By the way, when you play the B-flat horn you are using an instrument pitched a fourth higher than the F-side of the instrument. It is much shorter, therefore, easier to play in the higher register!! Notes a', b', and c" are all played the same way with either side of the horn…no problem! Usually, you switch from F-horn to the B-flat horn on second line g-sharp, which also has the same fingering for both horns! Now, if you want some of the other advantages of playing a double horn (which most young musicians don't need right away) you will have to learn a few more fingerings.

A brief run-down of other benefits that you derive from a little bit more study; extra power on low register for the same amount of effort, clever combinations of fingerings that simplify passages that could be cumbersome without alternate fingerings, and the ability to fill in the complete range of the instrument in that area where there are no legitimate tones on low F-horn. (And still lower when you run out of pedal tones on the B-flat horn…if you are willing and able and need to get that low!)

Most authorities ask that the mouthpiece be placed firmly, 1/3 on the lower lip, assuming that the upper lip will then be free to vibrate for maximum tone quality. For me, this is really the best position, and, also for me, the most satisfying condition for slurring effortlessly, up and down the full range of the instrument, using little but that "roar to a hiss" I shall mention for the 'umpteenth" time!

As noted before, it is not within the compass of this book to give all the details for the complete mastery of an instrument. However, I do hope to do a bit of a "selling" job where I feel it necessary and will include items that I have observed to be helpful. With that in mind, I want to mention a drill I like to use, which includes the fascinating effect you get when you "stop" the horn by "stuffing" your hand in the bell in such a way as to almost completely curtail the air movement. This is called "hand muting" and the pitch jumps either <u>up</u> or <u>down</u> a half step when you do it! There is considerable argument about which to use! Should you transpose <u>down</u> to get the correct pitch or <u>up</u>? I feel that some notes in some parts of the range sound better one way than the other so the individual performer shall have to make up his own mind about which to use.

There are other forms of mutes that you actually insert in the bell but that is not of interest here. Now, when "plus" signs are inserted over the notes, those tones are to be muted and you had better be ready to transpose <u>down</u> a half-step to allow for the transposition you get when you mute! Now, for the exercise I mentioned: I like to play an open "c" for example, then the muted "b," which will be the same pitch! Then play an open "b" and a muted B-flat, etc. At this point I could insert an asterisk for a foot-note and hope you don't read it, but, I'm going to admit here that I inadvertently, in my first edition, quoted how to mute just the opposite of what I intended! There, I said it! By the way, for some reason, after using the effort to play a good muted tone, you get one heck of a big tone when you follow it with the open tone! Careful now! You can overdo it and mess up your lip!

Hey, I guess I shouldn't have waited this long to mention right hand position in the bell! As we suggested what to do when first checking a flute player (the end plug) we also are immediately concerned about the hand position of a horn student! Boy, you catch them doing everything from hand in their lap, hand on top of bell, hand "stuffed" too far in, too far out, etc., on and on! Don't bend those fingertips up either! Instead, expect that you are purposely planning that your hand should provide a "fleshy" side to the bell. We learn in acoustics that the material surrounding the opening alters the tone quality. (This can be noticed in the pipes of a pipe organ where many different shapes and materials are used; wood, metal of various sorts and sometimes, even leather.) We really desire a warm, mellow sound unless the music calls for raised bells with a much harsher tone quality. Also, if you have your hand in the right spot, moving it in a bit will flat the tone, while moving it out will cause you to go sharp! This can be important for the polished performer. It can be noted that, before there were valves, capable artists could, by altering the hand position, navigate passages for which we now use valves!

Also, on the matter of horn position let us beware of the awkward "valves on top, bell pointed into the lap, head down to see the music" position usually found in a beginner. There is a great need to convince the student to cross the chest with the instrument, face the body a bit to the right on the chair, point the bell out the side, and above all, adopt a position that will enable him or her to keep that lower jaw firmly against the mouthpiece! Depending on the size of the student, the bell may be placed on the thigh or held, mid-air, which does allow for a freer vibration.

Tuning the French Horn can be time-consuming because you must tune _both_ sides of the horn to match each other as well as tune each slide of the horn to provide the best compromise of slide length for each valve. (The same considerations previously mentioned in the section on trumpet apply here.)

You want to play French horn? You had better be ready for properly maintaining it! Rotary valves must be kept in tip-top shape and are a bit more of a nuisance than those on other brass. At times the strings wear out or loosen. (See Appendix "C" for replacement Instructions.) Also, it is very important to check the limiters to valve motion. They wear and allow the valves to be misaligned with the tubing. This will be noticed by checking under the valve caps to see if the alignment marks are at the "notch" in _both_ positions of the valve. As you might expect, if the holes in the valves are not accurately aligned with the tubing, the tone and pitch will suffer.

Also, the levers need to be adjusted so all of them are at the same level…and all those slides! Wow! Keep them ready to move for tuning purposes. All of them have definite positions necessary in order for both sides of the horn to match! Also, they must be readily accessed so that moisture can easily be removed, as you would witness at a symphony performance when the horn section is constantly busy keeping those horns ready to play without a "bobble." "Good luck!" To help visualize the rotation necessary to remove moisture from tubing other than valve slides, I find it helpful to imagine a "marble" in the tube…now, "how should I rotate the instrument to make that marble run out of the tube?"

Oiling the rotary valves is not as easy as with the pistons on the rest of the brass family. My son-in-law, Karl Pituch, presently Principal Horn of the Detroit Symphony, had tiny holes drilled into the plate, which can be found under the bottom of the valve cap. This _is_ a clever solution to the problem, but he does advise that oil can be introduced through the various tuning slides, but to prevent oil from "washing" slide grease into the valves, _do_ pour oil into the _slide_ itself and then return the slide while still retaining the oil. Then, and only then, tip the horn so the oil runs onto the valve.

TROMBONE!

Well, well, a really different kind of instrument but, oh so, nice! And so important to that low brass section! First, great care should be taken to show a prospective player the sensible way to get the instrument in and out of the case! I can picture kids; slides in two pieces and a bell tucked under the arm in a strange direction with hands full of mouthpiece and instruction books! Here's the way to start! (1) Take the delicate slide out first. Be sure it is locked and "hang" it from your right hand. Make sure that the side you will fasten to the bell to is toward you. (2) Now pick up the clumsy bell that is not nearly so delicate…this we do in such manner that the bell is immediately in a position to go on the slide without further twisting and turning. (Hand should be in the proper position right when you remove the bell from the case.) (3) Position the bell so it is about equidistant from both sides of the slide, being very cautious to avoid "bumping" the slide, and fasten the bell securely with the threaded connector. (4) Now, and only now, should you retrieve the mouthpiece and twist it gently into place. None of that tapping just so you can hear that cute little "pop!" That is how mouthpieces get stuck! (Especially if they are bent, dirty, and without lubrication!) Put the horn away in absolutely reverse order and never hand the horn to someone unless you lock the slide!

We need good low brass but they so often have the most offensive tone quality, primarily because of that ugly "buzz" theory! We get good results almost immediately when we apply the methods outlined above! You don't even need to send the student home to practice long tones with all those instructions to listen carefully to your sound, etc. If they use that buzz on a low brass it will sound like it on the horn!

I had occasion one time to give a little clinic on percussion, and just as the session came to an end, in walked a sousaphone player proudly blowing what he considered a pretty good sound. Well, it was obvious he was using that objectionable "buzz" just referred to. I couldn't resist asking him to blow, without the mouthpiece, the kind of sound I have been recommending. He "caught on" immediately, and when he applied it to the horn he went delirious with joy at the tone he produced and told us he couldn't wait for school next day to demonstrate his new-found skill! This is what makes teaching such a pleasure!

We would like to stress again that tension all across the lips should be avoided! "Clench" at the edges of the mouthpiece and allow the portions of the lip in the mouthpiece to vibrate freely. I feel I should repeat the advice to allow the mouthpiece to rest rather firmly against the lower jaw, with perhaps two thirds of the mouthpiece on the upper lip, almost to the nose! The theory being that the major support is against the lower jaw with a lot of upper lip in the mouthpiece to vibrate freely for good tone quality. At this writing 12/30/2011, just gave a trombone lesson an hour ago. Mentioned tongue to be flat in bottom of mouth behind the tip of the tongue, which is behind the upper teeth…worked like a charm to make "clean" attacks, both single and double-tonguing! Information just "gleaned" from an internet article quoting Bary Tuckwell! Have a feeling this information could be used for every wind instrument!

Do not allow the fingers of the right hand to touch the bell at any time! You don't need that "crutch" for the other positions so don't use it for 3rd and 4th!

Learn to move the slide by bending the wrist to "throw" it out part way, using the forearm only for part of the motion. "Drag" the slide back, in combination with the "throwing" just mentioned. As soon as you get over the notion of moving the entire forearm when you change position, you will be much more efficient and, what is even more important, when it comes time to move that slide you will be able to do it at the last possible moment, and do it quickly! It will also be easier to stop it right where you want it!

Where shall we stop it? Our t-bone can be played so much more in tune than other brass if we listen carefully! You have heard that the fifth partial is flat and the sixth is sharp? We can see that if we play, for example, top line A-flat, C, E-flat. Just by buckling the knuckles a bit you can correct those pitches ever so delicately! (C a bit shorter and E-flat a bit longer than A-flat...easy, if you listen!) I have just become owner of a tuner that clamps to the bell. Wow! What a nice way to locate slide positions, especially the alternates! This tuner is called, "Snark."

Note names are so important for these low brass or they will never remember the difference between A-flat, A-natural, and E-flat, E-natural, for instance.

With lower lip and jaw and tongue as mentioned above, the range should not be a problem. We will need careful attention to that idea of tonguing while blowing if we are to approximate slurring that matches the other instruments, and also if we want a true legato song style.

Alternate positions are even more useful to the t-bone than other brass. For example, when playing high C, D, E-flat, it is senseless to play 3-1-3, especially since D in 1st position is apt to be flat! Expect to use 3-4-3 practically every time. Low F-C-F would be horrible if you go 1-6-1 but you don't even have to move the slide if you go 6-6-6! A bass trombone with F-attachment facilitates matters even more by allowing the use of a thumb key to enable you to play that 6th position C, in 1st position! How do you like that! Just "wiggle" your thumb and stay right in 1st position to jump from B-flat to C! Learn a few new positions and you save yourself a lot of problems but I have known many to own (and carry!) a horn with the attachment, AND NEVER USE IT!

For slide lubrication, I may be out of date but personally used cold cream and water, which involves carrying a little water supply 'cause the cold cream dries out sooner than oil. They may have some better products for the purpose now. (A German product, "Slide-O-Mix" is excellent!) Not only is a slide difficult to maneuver if not properly lubricated, but, the metal rubbing against metal is sure to cause serious wear. You do the checking, but for goodness sake, don't allow students to try to play on dry or even dented slides. Also, caution them about taking the slide apart. It is so vulnerable to damage then!

We shall conclude this section about brass instruments with an anecdote dating w-a-a-ay back! I had this terrific 6th grade trumpeter and I wanted, of course, to show him off at a concert. Well, about the time of the event he started to sound terrible. What do you suppose had gone wrong! Well, he had practiced so much that, when I looked through his mouthpiece, I COULD NOT SEE MUCH DAYLIGHT! Moral of the story! Clean and maintain those instruments! Incidentally, this young man, now about 64, is still performing, both here and abroad!

Well, I tried not to, but I just cannot resist adding this extra info about utilizing pedal tones to prepare a brass player for the upper register! Hard to believe...hard to understand but I have known about this for quite some time! Only recently I began some serious practice (trumpet) more or less as an experiment, and, wow, I think it is too beneficial to ignore! At first the sounds are hideous but, by golly, they do get better, and there is a good feeling in the embouchure that I never noticed before!

Do maintain your normal embouchure while "faking" fourth-line "F-3" (Bass clef) down to pedal "C-3." 1, 1-2, 2-3, 1-3, 1-2-3, then pedal "C-3," (open). In the harmonic series this would be called the "fundamental." Next, all the normal pedal tones down to 2-3 (low A-2-flat), then, finally, open "G-2" all the way down to "C-2." (Two octaves below middle "C-4"!) (Possible to go down to "F#-1!) This last octave, I must admit, I can't explain, unless it has something to do with a "closed pipe" like the pipe organ where they can make a 32' stop out of a 16' pipe by "stopping" the end of the pipe.

"Take it or leave it!" You should use lots of breath for all of this, but I am still being very cautious with the 86-year old "chops!" I am having real fun with what I am experiencing! Maybe this procedure will have value for others, too! A word of caution, however! Be sure to do a lot of resting between exercises!

Since we have taken the liberty to mention items you may consider "far out," how about this observation? I don't want to offend anyone, but referring back to embouchure, I wonder if you have ever noticed that, with a poor embouchure, lips turned outward too far, you do not have nearly as much need to use the water key as you do when you have a real good formation! How's that for trying to be diplomatic! Yep, when those lips are used the right way, ya' can't stop the flow!

CHAPTER FOUR: PERCUSSION!

Well, I only know a certain amount about percussion, but what I do know I'd like to share with you. For starters how about the grip of the snare drum sticks? Oh, what a pity to see a lack of control that comes from poor balance or lack of understanding of the grip that would enable you to drive the stick downward and likewise, provide a way of picking the stick up! The properly balanced stick will have the correct amount in front and back of the grip. Too much in front of the grip and the stick goes down readily, but is not going to come up properly. Too much in back of the grip, and it comes up too easily, but isn't too ready to go down. It's that simple, but so often ignored.

Now, the grip, so easy to demonstrate, but we must put this into words! For the right hand, between the thumb and index finger, the stick should be held in a "snug" manner. But if you shake the wrist up and down, the stick really "wobbles!" The last three fingers should stay in a convenient position under the sticks where they add additional control. The side of the index finger is used to drive the stick down, and the thumb picks it up! Don't allow that "loose" grip where the student can do little better than drop the stick with not enough control to rebound when necessary. If we use this grip for both hands, we call it the "matched" grip, which for a while was in vogue, but more and more, you will see the old-fashioned left hand grip (even more difficult to explain with text), namely a palm facing up with the stick between the thumb and the index finger. The third finger accompanies the index finger, leaving the fourth and fifth fingers tucked into the palm. With this grip, the thumb is responsible for driving the stick downward, while the little platform formed by the fourth finger picks it up.

Here is an exercise I like because it makes a habit of the main moves your muscles must make during drumming: (I will sneak in a little reference to amplitude here 'cause it will be necessary to raise stick high for loud and low for softer sounds!) This has nothing to do with playing closer to rims for soft, however! Begin with one stick. Hold it high. Play it and end up high! Play it again and end up low! Play it low and end up low! Play it low and end up high! Do the same thing with the other stick. You have now made all of the important physical moves that muscles make in simple drumming! This exercise deserves many repetitions! Notice how the amplitude of stick movement creates varying amounts of volume!

Next let us consider rebounding the sticks. If they are held properly, the index finger applies downward pressure (right hand), thumb doing the same (left hand), causing many rebounds, unless you have hand positions that allow you to pick the stick up before it bounces more than once! Get good at rebounding like this with both hands; then try alternating hands and, if you do it smoothly, you will be rewarded with what we consider a roll. The first tap is usually stronger than the rebound which will prevent you from having a really smooth roll so try this: If you know the tune to "You're in the Army Now," try to imitate that with your sticks, all in one hand or alternately when you are better at it. Actually, of course, the rhythm is "tuh"-1, tuh-2, tuh-1! (Sixteenth to dotted eight...dotted eighth being on the beat!) There are those who count this rhythm, "to-day, to-day, to-day" etc. and, with drummers I don't mind if they <u>do</u> use "a"-1, a-2, a-1, as a counting system. Anyway, the emphasis you get when you use this exercise will help you to play very even rebounds!

Now...sticking! Get organized! I like to start with the left, mostly because it matches the left foot when marching! How awkward to play with the right hand and left foot in simple drumming. Oh, when you are advanced you can probably feel comfortable left or right! Under no circumstance should you <u>neglect</u> to practice every rudiment starting with either hand! Did I say RUDIMENT?? Yes, do learn many of the combinations possible under the classification of rudiments. Notice, even in the simple paradiddle, L-r-l-l and R-l-r-r, you will begin to use the exercise from above (amplitude) as the L will be high and end up low, followed by r-l-l, all low, but the "r" will fly to the <u>up</u> position to begin the R-l-r-r! Please take the trouble to really understand this last sentence. So many try to play the necessary accent to begin a paradiddle without lifting the first stick high, trying to produce accent without the benefit of a higher stick! (Old time rudimental drummers, mostly English style, used to lift the stick to "eye" level!) By the way, don't be ashamed to use these old rudimental terms. Sure, the kids will think them silly at first, but in no time they will become accustomed to them, and benefit from them.

Now, the FLAM: Left stick high, right stick low. Check them both, then <u>play</u> <u>them</u> <u>at</u> <u>the</u> <u>same</u> <u>time</u> and end up with <u>right</u> <u>stick</u> <u>high</u> <u>and</u> <u>left</u> <u>stick</u> <u>low</u>! (Did you notice how you have been prepared to play high to low, low to high...now we use what we learned in that exercise!) <u>Before</u> <u>you</u> <u>play</u> <u>the</u> <u>second</u> <u>flam,</u> <u>be</u> <u>sure</u> <u>to</u> <u>check</u> <u>to</u> <u>see</u> that <u>the</u> <u>sticks</u> are <u>exactly</u> <u>where</u> <u>you</u> <u>want</u> <u>them</u> <u>before</u> <u>you</u> <u>allow</u> <u>yourself</u> <u>to</u> <u>play</u> <u>them</u>!

Again, let me caution you about possible embarrassment when students hear you use these "strange" names and syllables. As with so many new things in a person's life, there is need for a period of adaptation to unaccustomed events. (Students should hear the <u>sounds</u> a jazz conductor uses to convey <u>his</u> ideas of style, accent and rhythm to his band..."scobbie-doo-be-doo-duh"...etc.!) Don't be denied the helpful sounds and techniques for counting, style, articulation and accent just because some may "twitter" at first hearing!!!

Back to sticking! A good example of the use of high to low, etc. is L-l R-r as required in a 6/8-march style while playing quarter followed by an eighth. How often you will catch someone playing what we call hand-to-hand...LRL, which ruins the skipping flow of the rhythm that you get when you play L-l, R-r, L-l, R-r, etc.

It is sometimes desirable to have the student on all these percussion instruments, treat the surface of the drumhead or keyboard or chime as thought it is "hot" and you want to get the stick away before it gets burned! "Draw the tone out!" What a pity when the stick is allowed to dampen the very vibration you tried to set in motion! This brings to mind two instances where there often is faulty procedure! One, striking the tympani head in the center, producing a dull thud compared to the proper striking location about four inches from the rim, and two, striking a gong without first helping set it quietly in motion by gently stroking it until it is time for the big, impressive sound! Also, with tympani, insist that the performer is very conscientious about "dampening" the tones faithfully. Just watch a professional timpanist and you will see some real technique in this regard!

While we are at it, let's register a BIG complaint about bass drumming that is not "balanced" with the rest of the ensemble! Supposedly, a famous conductor was not satisfied until the drum was struck with a toothpick! An exaggeration, of course, but somewhat accurate! A description of what I prefer is to "feel" the sound rather than "hear" it! Many times you will notice a very good performance "drowned out" by aggressive bass drummers, especially when they are not damping properly.

Now, let's say you have mastered the rebounding we discussed earlier. How to apply those rebounds? Well, in a way it is easy if you adopt the following procedure: <u>Single</u> <u>stick</u> the roll, hand to hand, (l-r-L, r-l-R), then, <u>rebound</u>, honestly insisting that the hands repeat just what you did when single sticking, but <u>do</u> allow for only <u>one</u> rebound for each single stick <u>except</u> the <u>last</u>, which would be a single tap. Here we like to <u>close</u> and <u>open</u> the rudiment, which means simply, speed up on each repetition as fast as it can be controlled, then, slow down as slow as possible, (like putting the rudiment under a magnifying glass)!

An example, for a five-stroke roll: single stick l-r-L, r-l-R. Now when you rebound the first two sticks of each group, presto! You have a five-stroke roll! Notice I am using a capital letter for the third stroke to denote accent! If you were to count, "an-da-1, an-da-2" you would have the <u>single</u> <u>sticking</u> for a five-stroke roll, written an eight (rolled) tied to a quarter – the quarter note ON the beat. This is called a <u>normal</u> roll! Notice! If the requested roll is a quarter note, this calls for what we call an <u>inverted</u> roll where the accent is <u>on</u> the first stick, counted <u>1</u>-e-an, <u>2</u>-e-an! This is a fun roll to play…as we would put it into sound, we would say, "DEERY-ump!" As opposed to a normal roll where we would say, "derry-UMP!" Believe me, if you use the recommended procedure of, single stick hand to hand, rebound hand to hand, and close and open the rudiment, you will surprise yourself with your development!

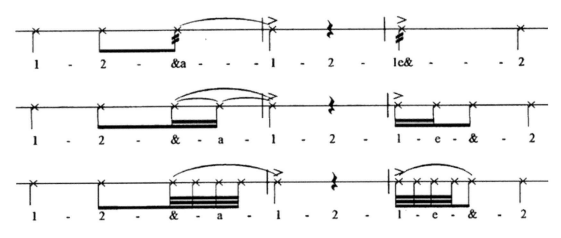

1st line (written) 2nd line (single stick) 3rd line (rebounded)
Be sure to accent as indicated

Before we discuss long rolls, lets see what you can do with a 9-stroke roll? DEERY-ery-UMP or deery-ery-UMP, written quarter-note on the beat, tied to an eighth, accented at the beginning <u>or</u> at the end according to the location in the measure. OK, do we have to tell you to single stick four sixteenths, hand to hand, then rebound, honestly using the same sticking? No cheating! What a shame to have a student do the single sticking perfectly, only to "fake" a roll by ignoring the rebound we cultivated so carefully!

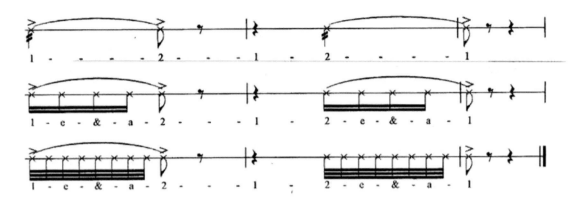

1st line (written) 2nd line (single stick) 3rd line (rebounded)

Now, for long rolls we simply singlestick the number of sixteenths we can play for the duration of the note! Now get this! If the long note is tied into the <u>next</u> beat, we rebound every single sixteenth and finish the roll with a tap! However, if the long note is <u>not</u> tied to the next beat, you must stop the rebounding earlier or it will sound like you rolled into the next beat, which is not what was desired in this case! A half-note rolled without the tie would then have single-sticking as follows: 1-e-an-duh-2-e-AN! We enjoy doing these and you will too! This then is opposed to the half-note roll that <u>is</u> tied to the next beat: 1-e-an-duh-2-e-an-duh-THREE! If you can't apply this to other long rolls of any other length, I feel sorry for your reasoning powers!

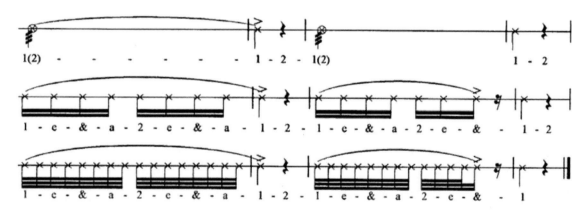

1st line (written) 2nd line (single stick) 3rd line (rebounded)

I was never introduced to the "drag roll" where the sticks are allowed to make multiple bounces contrary to the military style presented above. I call this to your attention here, advising you to explore other avenues for that kind of info.

Gee, we thought we were about finished with this section, but what about the triangle? I hate to hear the sound achieved when it is struck near the open end thus producing a "clanging" sound. I prefer the "sweet" tingling sound created when the triangle is struck ever so carefully <u>away</u> from the open ends. "Pull" the tone out – don't "bang" it in!

Maracas? Don't just shake them like a rattle! Use the rather complex motion that creates a centrifugal force to slide the seeds along the sides of the gourd instead of just bumping back and forth…sort of like making an arc of motion away and up from you and back again. Get it?

Cymbals? Be ever so careful in your selection of the size and weight of cymbals, and for goodness sake, have the performer aim with a "glancing" blow rather than too directly at each other. Don't make "Mickey Mouse ears" after a cymbal crash…the sound really comes off the edges of cymbals held one above the other in a horizontal position facing the listener. Also, be sure they are stopped abruptly against the body if a cutoff is in order rather than allowing them to ring unless that is the desired effect. I don't understand why it is so necessary and proper to have melodic instruments cut off together only to have the cymbals be allowed to keep ringing!

Chimes? About forty-five years ago a college band borrowed my prized set of chimes, and when they were returned the tubes were dented 'cause some band member hadn't been taught to strike them with a firm hammer blow to the "cap" at the top of the chime! Again, "pull" the sound out…you are not pounding a rail! Also, we certainly want to have a fine balance between the ensemble and the chime tone. They are so beautiful when played with a nice touch at the necessary dynamic level. What a pity to <u>not</u> hear them clearly on those relatively few occasions when they are called for!

Claves? How often the tone quality is dampened because the clave is not held properly. The thumb and index finger should provide the grip with the rest of the fingers and palm shaped in such manner that there is a resonating chamber for the lightly held clave. If done properly this will result in a very distinct, penetrating tone quality that greatly surpasses the dull "thud" you get from a faulty grip.

We leave you to your own devices as to the use of pitched percussion, castanets and the tambourine. (Show off with that thumb roll, if you can!)

Here is a tip I discovered too late to use in a selection that needed very fast back-time on the snare drum. At the side of the drum, unheard (on the thigh if you like) tap the downbeat with one hand, and the after-beat on the drum with the other! Wow, no matter how fast the tempo, you get an impeccable performance! Also, consider having your percussionists breathe at the beginning of phrases (just like wind instruments do) to enhance their sense of expression!

Gee, now that I think of it, there <u>is</u> a <u>lot</u> going on in that back row of the ensemble! A lot that can enhance your performance or destroy it! Those folks deserve much of our attention, (especially when they are NOT playing)!

CHAPTER FIVE: STRING BASS?

Yes, I did use a question mark in the heading for this chapter. You might not be one to appreciate the acoustic bass in a band but there are those who believe that there is something to be gained in tone quality when a string bass is added to the wind ensemble. In addition, if you form a jazz band, the string bass is desirable!

So, let's consider you are sold on the idea! Let's also hope you can find one available without having to pay the outrageous price of a new one! I prefer the German bow because it seems to give you a bit more tone although it is not quite as maneuverable on rapid passages. In addition, I prefer the German bow position when you shift to pizzicato tones. Be sure to check the proper method of holding the German bow. This is very important but I don't feel I can adequately describe the position in writing these instructions. (Basically, allow the bow to "dangle" downward with the thumb on the "stick" side and the little finger on the opposite side. Now, rotate the palm until it is under the bow.)

If your strings are not "false" (unusually worn) it is desirable to tune by harmonics because the low pitches can be difficult to match adequately. Get your "A" harmonic half way up the "A" string and compare it with the "A" you get one-third the way up the "D" string. Now, get the "D" half way up the "D" string and compare it with the "D" you get one-third the way up the "G" string, etc.

It is advisable to adjust the end-pin so that the "nut," the fitting at the upper end of the strings, is about at the level of your eyebrows. Very important for left hand strength is the positioning of the thumb opposite the <u>third</u> finger, <u>not</u> pointing upward away from the fingers. You will notice this hand position causes you to have a raised elbow. You will tire more readily if you try to exert the necessary pressure on the strings without having this advantage. With bass, as opposed to violin and cello, we use 1st, 2nd and 4th fingers, especially in the lower positions. A good left bass hand almost naturally adopts this position if you open your palm and stretch your fingers. You will observe a "gap" between the first and second fingers.

There is a recommended style that should be observed when playing bass parts. <u>Almost never</u> should the notes be connected in a legato manner. The bow is to be stopped <u>on</u> the string. This provides us with a "clean" bass line. Even when playing pizzicato it is customary to stop the tones in most cases. (Tuba players could profit by using the same technique.)

And…keep those strings clean! A buildup of rosin that dries and hardens is not conducive to fine tone quality.

Again, be on the lookout for a "dropped elbow" on the novice player! If the left elbow is not kept in the raised position, the fingers of the left hand will be weaker because the thumb will not be right under the third finger for maximum power.

I so often notice people, even "pros," carrying their basses and cellos in such an awkward manner, especially when in a group of people, such as after a performance when everyone is hurrying to the parking lot and up stairways, etc. May I suggest placing the neck of the instrument on, say the right shoulder, strings outward and the right hand, in this case, slipped under the top edge of the inner bout of the instrument.

I hesitate to go back to see if I mentioned this previously, but I also like to carry my trombone in a vertical position with the bell tucked in front on my shoulder, right hand in the grip down at my side. This avoids having a long case protruding from the front and the back, especially when in a crowd, on a bus or similar situation.

CHAPTER SIX: BEGINNING BAND!

FOURTH GRADE!

The most common start for the school music program is about May of fourth grade. This is the time for showing interest, having a parental meeting, getting tested and relatively soon getting "fitted" for an instrument. There could be later meetings for students who may still want to become part of the beginning band in fifth grade. Much of this is organized with the help of businesses that sell instruments and music as well as provide repair facilities.

A few words of caution are in order at this stage:

1. Testing can be valuable for many reasons, but students with high motivation should not necessarily be denied training purely on the basis of test scores.
2. Which instrument is promoted for an individual should not be based primarily on "fitting" since the preference so often is determined by other factors.
3. It is usually not advisable to force a student to play a certain instrument just because a "second hand" instrument is available. For example: If "daddy" has an old trumpet lying around, a kid wanting to play a flute is not apt to accept the idea…very nice if they will, but so often not in the best interest of the child.
4. Beware of the attempt by merchants to sell some of the larger and more costly instruments that could justifiably be provided by the music department.
5. As mentioned in a previous chapter, be cautious about purchasing Single French Horns. Later, a serious student, no doubt, will find that he requires the Double Horn.
6. Don't let anyone demand rental of a new instrument if an individual already has an adequate instrument available.
7. Consider starting a potential tuba player on a school-owned baritone if it is not immediately practical to use a tuba. (Use tuba instruction book.)
8. Instrument sales representatives promise balanced instrumentation, which is so desirable, but too much emphasis on this needs to be overseen so that, for the most part, the youngsters are playing what they prefer.

CLASS BEGINS! (Hopefully in fifth grade!)

Perhaps by the second week of school all is in readiness for beginning instruction. A large, beginning class can be taught most efficiently if scheduling is possible somewhat as follows:

1. Monday – Flutes and oboe
2. Tuesday – Clarinets
3. Wednesday – Saxophones
4. Thursday – All Brass
5. Friday – Percussion (Later in year – full ensemble)

CLASS PROCEDURE!

If possible a lot of piano accompaniment is really beneficial because, right from the beginning, pitch is established. Also, some of the "agony" of beginning sounds is compromised so everyone feels more at ease.

The technique of having students volunteer to "demonstrate" as the class progresses also provides useful incentive.

Do not neglect to emphasize care of the instruments, especially how to place them if they want to put them down temporarily. Ugh! What a risk it is to stand a clarinet on its bell…a flute across a music stand…a trombone unlocked, with the bell on the chair, etc.

Special attention can "save" a slow starter on any of the instruments. Students must be made aware of the need to adjust, which for some takes a bit longer than for others. Everyone needs to know that, how you do in the beginning is no true indication of what you will be able to accomplish later!

Especially try to help those who have a problem getting the correct pitch required in the beginning pages of the lesson book. Let them know that someone who cannot get "high enough" or "low enough" on the brass will eventually be perfectly capable of playing the notes desired. <u>No one must judge what he or she will later be able to do on the basis of his or her first attempts</u>!

I am reminded of a strange instance in which a trumpet student, early on, had to quit because his father tried to blow the horn and had difficulty, as might be expected, whereupon he decided if <u>he</u> couldn't do it, neither could his child!

You might observe that a beginning brass player, being understandably "anxious," will "try so hard" that the tongue is tight and raised, which causes poor results. You might asks the student to make believe they are playing, without the horn, and you may find that they are striving for a pitch much higher than the one desired. This prevents the relaxation needed for nice tone production at this stage.

I would like to suggest that, if you have the time and talent, write an "alto" part for your French Horn students. The range required for these poor kids is either much higher or much lower than convenient, and it is not the worst thing for them to begin to hear harmony at this stage. So often it is discouraging for these students to need pitches that are relatively difficult to attain, while other students have the most favorable beginning register on their instruments

Stress "posture." I purposely selected chairs that "sloped" forward a bit to counteract the tendency for students to lean against the back. At least, instruct the students to position one foot in front of the other in such manner that they can stand up <u>without</u> having to move the feet! This is a good "trick" to use for attaining desirable posture. However, as mentioned earlier in this book, even with leaning against the chair back, it is possible to experience proper and adequate breathing if the "small" of the back is projected forward, away from the chair!

I prefer to attempt a "legato" approach to playing right from the start by having the students learn to tongue "while blowing." This avoids that disconnected style that some don't ever seem to overcome and it <u>is</u> conducive to nice rendition of the little songs they will soon play, not to mention getting the trombones ready for the style they will need when the rest of the class learns to slur.

Pay lots of attention to the way the instruments are held, even if some require lots of conditioning before it will seem natural. Also, the posture must be monitored if successful breathing is to take place. As early as possible you can introduce some of the many appropriate concert arrangements that have been tailored expressly for this beginning band of yours. Don't neglect this opportunity to provide fun and incentive for your kids! Good luck! Be proud of the ability to give these youngsters a happy, enjoyable introduction to music performance!

CHAPTER SEVEN: REHEARSAL PROCEDURE!

PLANNING!

When you consider rehearsal planning, first think of public performance! After all, that is the purpose for rehearsing, we would assume! This leads us immediately to give consideration to what is appropriate to present. Sounds almost ridiculous to mention this, but I am very concerned about the audience, and you should be too! For my taste, a concert should not be too "heavy" for the particular audience you expect to have. In our school situation, contrary to that of the professional orchestras, we do not have the luxury of providing "Pop concerts" <u>and</u> concerts of strictly "serious music! Our concerts should therefore strike a balance between various styles and even include featured performers if possible. Simply stated, there should be lots of variety! And, for goodness sake, some of the music should be familiar! One of my pet peeves is to attend a concert where applause is just somewhat "polite" during the program only to become really generous at the end upon finally hearing something familiar as an encore!!!

Next, we should be practical enough to select material, comfortably within the range of the skills of the ensemble, and something <u>they</u> will enjoy. Surely, it helps to select some compositions that "stretch" their ability and hopefully are suited to the particular strengths of the group. And—don't make that program too long! Rather leave the audience wishing you had played more, instead of, "I thought it would never end!"

I may as well mention here that I think a concert should be a "Happening!" Recently I attended a Christmas concert where the only decorations were two little wreathes off to the sides of the stage with electric cords hanging down, and… they forgot to light them!

> **"I love atmosphere! Can't live without it!"** (D'ya' get it?)
> Heffelfinger

In addition to taking a cue from symphonic concerts by providing a featured soloist, sometimes it can be worth the effort to "dress up" a production. For example, when doing a selection with narration such as "Night Before Christmas," why not have a student "reader" in a rocker, holding a little child to read to…climaxed by giving the child a gift! Did this once and the little kid 'exploded' into action, ripped off the wrapper, and created an unforgettable scene, to the obvious delight of the audience! (If you are interested in another concert "gimmick," see Appendix "E," "Snowman!"!

Provide nice programs (so easy to make with today's computers) and nice posters, well in advance, if only to let the participants in the concert feel pride in preparing for such a presentation! If possible, newspaper coverage could aid in anticipation of the event. I have lately become aware of the fact that resumés are enhanced if students can include programs that give them due recognition of their musical accomplishments. "Skimpy" programs aren't too beneficial!

Seasonal performances certainly provide the opportunity for decorations…risers give momma and papa, who pay the bills, a chance to see more than the top of their kid's heads and also enhance the performance by allowing rear sections to project without the customary muffled tone. (Don't be too lazy to build your own…plans follow in Appendix A.) Recently saw a good idea for letting the audience recognize the participants at the end of a performance when no risers were available…let the students rise, one row at a time, starting at the rear…very effective, I thought!

Incidentally, if you do build risers of the type described in Appendix A, expect that other groups in the school will want to use them, especially Jazz Band, Pep Band and often Drama Clubs, etc. (Beware…once had some Thespians "customize" some of our risers with a saw!)

Consider flattering lighting if available. Me…I've had enough of going to concerts under fluorescent lights with banks of pretty, colored "gels" on the border lights, available, and <u>unused</u>! Also, with dimmers presently available on lighting boards, avoid the "podunk" theater effect you get when lights go on and off abruptly!

Those who may be "stuck" with setting up chairs for the concert audience, consider a plan I thought very effective for my concerts. Instead of lining chairs in a row like soldiers on parade, I swung an arc from the conductor's podium and "curved" the rows as they are in most auditoriums! This creates a setting where all people face directly at the stage, rather than having to look sideways, and it also allows a friendly atmosphere where people see each other in the audience, across the rows, instead of merely feeling closed in between the two people beside them!

Did you notice the importance I place upon concert preparations, beyond the playing of music? If possible, I would like to appeal to <u>all</u> the senses, even the sense of smell! (Especially during those years when I had to set up a <u>gym</u> <u>floor</u> for a concert one or two hours after basketball practice!)

If you don't mind, I will now get down to the business of rehearsal! I prefer to have some classical music playing as the group enters the room and turn it down as the students are gradually ready to warm-up. We want the class to realize that our love of music goes beyond just concert band or orchestra. (Even include opera selections 'cause I want my students to respect vocal musicians as well as instrumentalists.)

Now, this might <u>not</u> strike you as good technique, but my groups were prepared (6th grade and JH) to play any number of songs from collections, and at the beginning of a period while I was attending to the sometimes unending distractions faced by all teachers, the group displayed its independence and degree of responsibility by agreeing on a selection from their many favorites, and away they would go! I was proud of them for being self-governing, regardless of the size of the band. One number concluded and there would be momentary haggling, and finally they would strike up another! Now, consider this: Many times I felt that they played better then, than they did when I was conducting! You see, they <u>had</u> to <u>listen</u> to each other under those circumstances!

With this technique, classes were off to a quick start without me and I think they were learning a valuable lesson of cooperation. No lost playing time…no individual loafing or slowly getting ready…no student "showing off" with harmful over-blowing!

Next, we come to a "fork in the road of rehearsal procedure!" You can have an extended warm-up of scales, rhythm patterns and chorales…then tune! Or, immediately work on music and teach that which you require through the process of rehearsing music!

Personally, I felt I needed every possible moment I could get for preparing the music and probably should have devoted more time to disciplined warm-up. Maybe the best course would have been a little bit of both approaches, but, in either case, don't short-change the tune up!

Tuning! Hey, let's start from the bottom up. It is worthwhile to consider balance, tone, and tuning by getting the low tuba's first…next the baritones and trombones and F-horns, low woodwinds…then saxes, and on up through the top of the band. May we introduce the reasoning here: Remember the harmonic series! Well, it is desirable to have the upper instruments tuning to the partials that are produced by the tuba. We know that each tone possesses, in addition to the fundamental, harmonics an octave higher, then a fifth, another octave, then the third, fifth, etc. How could the sound be desirable if the upper instruments played pitches that did not "match" these partials produced by the lowest instruments?

CLASSROOM MANAGEMENT!

Let us digress a bit to make some suggestions that might seem obvious to some but helpful to especially that teacher who may have thought that a thorough knowledge of music is the main prerequisite! Welcome to the real world of teaching! We hope you have a sense of humor and are not so overly concerned about discipline that you are hesitant to use it! (The "humor," that is!)

1. A few don'ts: Don't be afraid to admit you don't know – admit it, then promise to find out!
2. Don't try to "fake it" if in error! They will know if you're trying! Own up to it and move on.
3. Don't yell, scream or belittle students! It doesn't help matters! Don't do it!
4. Don't "play favorites."
5. Don't let interruptions to your routine get you down…there will be fire drills, pep assemblies, field trips, snow days, in-service days, etc.
6. Do face the inevitable! Rise above the frustrations. Be positive and try to overcome all obstacles! In spite of everything, enjoy yourself! Be enthusiastic! Have fun with the music and the students!

"Friendship and respect are based on understanding."
(Sorry, author unknown to me!)

A word of caution, however! If you are successful, you will probably be admired, but don't join the ranks of those who allow their position to unduly influence their close relationship with students. More directors seem to lose their employment for reasons of imprudent behavior than for lack of musical teaching skills!

Before I proceed, I do have two items somewhat related to classroom management that deserve to be dealt with: namely, music library and fund-raising.

If you inherit an unkempt library, it will be very time-consuming to fully organize. Under certain circumstances it might be worth considering just plain ignoring what is already in place because so much of it you will probably never use. Whichever portions of the available music you find usable could be added to the new material you acquire and I would call your attention to filing methods you might find advantageous.

First, unless you have oodles of storage space, avoid alphabetical listing because the first time you buy new music you will have an obsolete list and placing it in position on shelves or in drawers will necessitate cramming it into a space which you may not have anticipated.

A card file where you simply assign a number to a selection enables you to locate music readily as well as making it possible to place music in storage in numerical order so you don't have wasted space as you would if you filed alphabetically. You may find it desirable to file music in separate categories such as: Overtures, Concert Marches, Christmas Selections, Jazz Band, Solos/Band Accompaniment, etc.

Serious thought should be given to your Solo & Ensemble materials. There are so many categories to file, including selections for each of the instruments, and all of the possible combinations of instruments. In addition, some selections have piano accompaniment. Be sure it is all accounted for!

In any event, do adopt a filing system and stick to it! Keep it up to date or you will waste a lot of time (and music and money)!

I just recalled a system for year-end collecting of music that you might find helpful. Rather than saddle some music librarian with the odious task of sorting and placing scads of music in score order, etc., I placed the names of all the songs in my folio (and there would be many) on the blackboard in any order. Then, and this is important, have every folder accounted for with students "covering" every folio (in case of absences) and have each student place all their parts in the order you wrote them on the blackboard. Next I use tables and chairs and what ever to put my scores where the students can walk by, in single file, and place their parts on mine. Start with the percussion and so on up through the instrumentation list and, in almost no time at all, everything is sorted and in score order ready to be filed! How do you like that!

Now, the second item: Fundraising! You must be willing to add to what the administration can provide! Don't be helpless in this regard. I, not being too good at delegating authority, organized too much of this myself...but it certainly was worth it! Active music parents can assume a great deal of this responsibility if you foster it. But, no matter who does it, get it done! How nice it is to have some items, readily available, which will help make your program successful,! If you really want results you will have to find ways to instigate action beyond that of the administration, even though they may already be very cooperative.

I hesitate to give advice about specific methods of fund-raising...some methods are better than others...and there are many to consider. Let us just be content to make you aware of the extreme desirability of expecting to be involved with this facet of the job in order to have a fine music department.

ON WITH OUR PREPARATIONS!

All right! Now we are standing in front of that ensemble – any age group. What kind of instrumentation do you have available? It had better be heavy in low brass with successively lighter quantities as you ascend to the soprano instruments! You cannot have a true quality ensemble without this distribution of instruments!

One of the first things I like to hear, after tuning, is a chord built from the bottom up. Start with the tubas (no percussion, please)! Add the baritone and trombone…then low woodwinds, saxophones, horns, trumpets, clarinets and finally flutes. Do not add instruments until those that are sustained are pleasantly balanced (and tuned). Finally, stop the chord and ask the group to remember how much of a contribution they were making and use that volume to begin the chord together! What a lovely sound you get in this manner! Using the same balanced chord, try volume changes of all sorts…doesn't hurt to have group learn to respond to your conducting in this manner, either! (Where did I ever hear…in this situation, the clarinets above c" should never play louder than "mf"?)

Now, can we strike that same balance if we articulate some rhythm patterns…and if we play consecutive chords in a chorale! (Good old *"Treasury of Scales!"* Use it! Four-part chorale-style harmonization in every key with all sections getting a chance to play the scale!) (See bibliography.)

What we have been emphasizing here is the necessity to avoid "top heavy" instrumentation. There are often more treble instruments than we need! I feel sorry for the folks who therefore have to hold back their intensity, but in no way can you have the required beauty of tone in an ensemble unless you conquer this problem of balance! Which brings me to my next topic:

INSTRUMENT TRANSFER!

If mom and pop will allow it, you can rather quickly profit by having some of those unwanted flute, clarinet, and trumpet players switch to instruments you need so badly!

Students and parents willing, there are many advantages to switching, besides insuring a better instrumentation for your group, and it's up to you to sell the idea! Allow me to try to help you with the arguments you may need!

    1. It is very possible to become fairly proficient in any switch of instruments because the big task for a music student is to learn the fundamentals of music reading! The ability to play one instrument or another is relatively easy compared to that! This is why, in college, a music education student can learn to play two, and sometimes three, kinds of instrument in a semester or two!
    2. The new instrument in question could possibly be a school owned instrument, thus, no additional cost to the parent.
    3. Many students are properly proud to be able to play secondary instruments, much as their admired instructors do!
    4. There is a feeling of responsibility that is engendered in that person who actually responds to a desire to help make his ensemble successful by contributing what is obviously needed rather than providing a less needed instrument in the group.
    5. The primary instrument need not be completely neglected, as it can be helpful to perform in other ensembles, large or small, where his or her instrument can legitimately be needed.

I personally have "switched" percussion, clarinet, sax and flute to low brass, tuba, baritone, French horn (double), and including trombone with very satisfying results (and am very proud of the small amount of time required to do this).

OK, now we have that balanced group we so desire and require! Once that balanced chord has been attained, how about trying to achieve that same balance, note-to-note, measure-by-measure throughout a march!

Let's make it clear at this point that, thus far I have been thinking in terms of full ensemble, chord by chord. (Again I recommend *Treasury of Scales* by Leonard Smith...my favorite, No. 19!) In arrangements where instrumentation is necessarily changed to add variety, obviously the balance is changed to suit the requirements of the arranger or composer.

Now, back to our march! Here is a fine opportunity to introduce the need to take turns being important in the ensemble. The moving voice must be heard clearly, and, it should not have to "fight" to be heard over voices that are sustaining chords! It should be obvious that, when the accompanying voices are too loud, the moving voice will try to be heard by playing still louder...and the result is...NOISE!

In many instances I find it helpful to have long, accompanying tones attacked and then immediately dropped in volume so as to avoid covering the moving voices. This is not to imply that you use a "sfz" attack, but instead simply play the long tones at two different levels of intensity so that, at first the chord is easily recognized, but then immediately becomes subservient to the voice that is more important at the moment.

Now we repeat our desire to have musicians play "marcato!" If this has already been covered in another section, forgive me, but I think the information bears repeating! Some think that an accent mark means strike the note heavily. This is usually true when an occasional accent is over a single note, but when there are successive accent marks, "marcato" is the intended style! This style is often described as having "daylight" between the tones. The notes are held as long as possible without connecting to the following tones. This is not too easy to acquire and every single member of the ensemble must develop the skill because one student playing "legato" would ruin the effect! Care must be taken to avoid making the notes too short. We do not want staccato in this case. When and if tones are stopped together properly, it creates an effect that students immediately recognize and appreciate! (And so do those "judges" at a festival!) It is well worth the effort to develop a fine marcato style!

Since we have been discussing style, let's caution you about the quarter followed by an eighth in 6/8 marches. This rhythm should really be played as though it were written "eighth note, eighth rest, eighth note." The music would look very "cluttered" if it were written that way, so, to be very practical, we write it as follows, recognizing that the rhythmic figure sounds much better with proper separation of the notes:

(Written) (Played)

FESTIVAL PREPARATION!

My first thought when I approached this topic was, "Oh, how often too much emphasis on festivals limits the amount of literature that will be experienced in the course of the school year!" I, too, would like the reputation of getting all those straight "I" ratings, but...at what cost to the opportunity for us to play lots of different music? Unless you are extremely capable, "ya' pays yer money and ya' makes yer cherce!"

I have known of situations where the first classes of the school year were devoted to beginning work on the required festival march to be used <u>six</u> <u>months</u> <u>later!</u> A further example: Christmas concerts with "festival music" and, just a <u>token</u> amount of the voluminous amounts of literature that is appropriate at that season! Further; mid-season concerts with nothing but a <u>short</u> program, a dress rehearsal of…you guessed it…festival music! Then, you made it to the State Festival! Congrats! Now you can practice some more "festival music!" Finally the time for a Spring Concert arrives and, for part of the program…some "festival music!" As you often hear these days, "Give me a break!" What happens to all the beautiful possibilities of having those students enjoy more of the wonderful arrangements available today? There is so much to choose from, and so many other styles to experience, and so much more that mama and papa would enjoy hearing their little darlings present!

If you are capable of both succeeding with festival competition, <u>and</u> adequately fulfilling the requirements of well-rounded concert presentations <u>plus</u> satisfying the public…then, HOORAY! On the other hand, if you must make a choice, let's have it be in favor of the latter. Incidentally, it is a pity if a music program is developed almost solely for the benefit of a director who wants to use it as a "stepping stone" to a "higher goal!" (An all too frequent occurrence.)

In your efforts to do well at festivals, and this applies to Solo & Ensemble as well as the full ensemble, do select your music with great care. Your success depends on quality of performance and not so much on degree of difficulty! To select the most impressive music you are capable of playing well is an art in itself. Nothing is gained by trying to play material beyond the grasp of the ensemble. I have visions of the multitude of depressed students standing by the cafeteria when the ratings are posted…victims of attempting music too difficult! "Pride cometh before a fall!" You, as director, have the responsibility to make judicious choices!

Unfortunately, a lot of attention must be paid to the performance conditions you are apt to face. A band accustomed to an auditorium will probably be too "noisy" in a gym! Offend the judges with anything "louder than lovely," and you will not be rewarded. Conversely, if your practice facilities are "live" and you are to perform in an auditorium you can be "swallowed up" by the completely different acoustics! Sometimes a position closer to the front of the stage can be advantageous. (There are times when the opposite may be true.)

At this moment in my writing, exclamation points are not strong enough to convey the extent of my emotional disturbance when I see an unprepared "set-up crew" fumbling about the stage!! What must the judges think! True, when we hosted a festival, and a director and assistant came, days in advance, from 50 miles away, to measure our stage (during school hours), I thought it a bit much! But I think some serious planning <u>must</u> be devoted to this facet of festival competition! Organize a real efficient "set-up crew!"

The band that does <u>not</u> pay lots of attention to frequent "tuning" will suffer if adjustments are made at the last critical moment. Musicians are so adaptable that they will almost naturally learn to "favor" the pitch of their instruments, and once they have made all those adjustments, last minute tuning will destroy much of what they accomplished.

By the way, have you ever noticed those long lines of band members waiting in the hallway for their entry to the performance area? What a pity to do all that warm-up and tuning, and then allow those instruments to "cool off!" (Especially the bigger brass.) It is only reasonable to suggest that students breathe a bit of warm air into those horns while they wait, especially since they sometimes are in the relatively cold halls for a considerable length of time.

Sight-reading capability is another item that had better not be neglected till the last minute. Assuming careful training in the early stages of instruction, confidence and procedure needs to be developed and experienced. Two items so often problematical are: (1) Counting rests, and (2) Wrong notes because of ignored key signatures. Almost as serious is inattention to dynamics. Judges love to hear dynamic changes! Give them lots of that and while you're at it, please try to provide excellent intonation!

One unforgettable director I knew folded his arms and didn't say <u>one word</u> during the seven-minute preparation time…then, without uttering a sound he would direct a First Division performance of sight-reading! Now, if you don't think you or your group can handle that, you need a good, efficient way to utilize your preparation time. I would recommend having lots of student involvement in the process. <u>They</u> tell <u>you</u> the meter, dynamics, key signature, and repeats. (They can see this on their music more readily than you can "fumble" through a score!) Then, a real run-through, vocalizing pitch and rhythm and dynamics to the best of their ability, all the while making believe they are playing their instruments. Needless, to say, in the interest of conserving preparation time, the director should reserve the right to skip portions or repeats he considers unnecessary. Good luck with your festival, *but don't you ignore those folks at home!*

ON WITH THE REHEARSAL!

Well now, let's just read our way through from one end to the other to see just what may be needed to make this composition acceptable in the "eyes and ears" of the beholder, whether it's the instructor, the students, the parents, or finally the judges we so often prepare for!

For my taste, after that first reading, it may be quite some time before we will ever read from beginning to end again! I have often heard students mention at concert time that they didn't feel as though they ever played the entire selection non-stop! (And it may have been true!)

I much prefer to stop just about every time there is something to correct. This can be a real pain to those who may have been counting measures only to have the process come to a halt just as they were ready to become involved! But, and I have long detested this expression, there are some directors who often say, "Take it from the top!" What a waste of time and energy!

By stubbornly following this procedure (stopping to correct) we all get a feeling that we are really gradually "getting somewhere." My proof of the value of this approach is that my groups traditionally did not get tired of playing a selection, even before they have fully prepared it! It is motivational to finish a day's work and be able to point with pride to a fairly polished section rather than to have that uneasy feeling that none of it is very well done, yet! It <u>does</u>, however, make sense to finish a rehearsal on a positive note by playing something already fairly well prepared by the group.

Proudly, I recall, upon retiring, my band, directed by a friend, replayed our entire Spring Concert, while I just sat and listened; all of this on a day when they weren't even required to report to school. They <u>still</u> were not tired of the music! In fact, very recently students, of as much as 50 years ago, have been pleased to receive recordings of selections they played back in the '60's and '70's! (Now converted to CD's, of course!) And they are not tired of the selections, even now! (Sorry to say, some directors don't have their groups play enough music in a year to fill a "CD!") Recently, we have begun enjoying fellowship with alumni who meet with us to have "playing reunions" with former students! (Some from the early '50's to the present!) This, I highly recommend! Facebook made it all possible to organize!

This brings me to the subject of recording! Oh, how I valued this facet of our work! What a pity to prepare a group and have their efforts gone forever immediately after the concert! But I am getting off the subject a bit! When I mention recording, I am referring to the moment when some of our music is prepared well enough to put on tape. I like to do a lot of classroom recording, not so much to play back to the class each time, but for me to study at my leisure. My best work has <u>always</u> been done when I attempted to make the performance good enough to sound satisfactory on a <u>recording</u>! That becomes my "measuring stick!" I think most directors will admit that they notice more when they listen to a recording than is possible while conducting.

While I am on the subject, consider this technique of recording: assuming you have some good "microphones" and have room to place them a reasonable distance from the group, put both "mics" together, aiming at each other on one stand, and at an angle so each "mic" covers the opposite side of the group. Then…have you ever wondered why you don't get satisfactory results with your recording? Maybe you have the trumpets so close that the high brass is dictating the recording volume! In this case the low instruments, usually in the back of the set-up, don't have a prayer of coming through sufficiently!

In a classroom, place the trumpets as far away as you can and place the rest of the ensemble in locations where a volume check will ensure that they will be duly represented in the recording process! You may be amazed at the quality you get that you didn't think possible with your equipment! This may look odd in a concert set-up, but the concert will be over and done with…and the recording will endure! As a side note, I will mention that years ago, Dr. Revelli took one look at the seating chart on my record jacket and severly chastised me for using such a poor arrangement, not realizing that we relied on that seating to provide the best recording opportunity.

If you <u>do</u> get motivated to make CD's of your ensemble, gee whiz, go to the trouble of providing meaningful information on your record jackets! I have seen all too many records (even of high quality) with no seating chart, much less appropriate pictures and perhaps even comments regarding the year's activity. (Our 1970 recording, in addition to pictures of all the seniors, and the aforementioned seating chart, even had the prediction that we would possibly be able to enjoy hearing ourselves in the year 2000…and what do you know…WE DID!) A trombone player in this group, Don McMonagle, later became an astronaut (4 missions, last as commander of the flight). I had sent him the CD and received a phone call from him while on his trip from Texas to Florida. He had ignored the CD until he was bored enough to slip it in, not really expecting too much and; the reason for the call, he was so excited to hear the quality that he said the hair stood up on the back of his neck! Bet it didn't even do that when he made his first flight! We are justifiably proud of our association with Don (had us come to Florida to witness his first flight…now, proud to say, has one of our schools named in his honor!).

I will mention again that I felt I did my best work when I bothered to study my recordings. It was so easy to determine what to emphasize in subsequent rehearsals. Also, and this might be considered to be a bit 'sneaky,' but, if you do a lot of recording, your ensemble gets accustomed to the discipline necessary for sustained effort at a high concentration level. It doesn't hurt a bit for a class to have that extra pressure to play their parts well enough to avoid possible embarrassment upon playback! A word of caution: some students may disturb the normal balance when the recorder is on because they make a conscious attempt to make sure they hear their part above that of others whether or not that is desired!

You may have noticed that I am not fond of too much percussion! Having an appreciation of classical music which consists of mostly orchestra and opera, I naturally want an ensemble to have a similar quality with the percussion serving to just "season" the rich sound of the wind instruments, unless, of course, the percussion is to be featured, in which case, "let 'er rip!"

This attitude toward percussion <u>does</u> cause a need for extra consideration to be given to the morale and behavior of the percussionists! However, I really prefer to do a lot of rehearsing without the percussion, only adding that after we hear acceptable performance by the rest of the ensemble!

CHAIR POSITION!

Let me once again demonstrate how unorthodox I can be at times! <u>I</u> <u>don't</u> <u>like</u> <u>fighting</u> <u>for</u> <u>first</u> <u>chair</u>! (First year of teaching, I had two flutes sitting right under my baton, who hated each other because of the competition for chairs, a procedure used by an earlier director!) You go right ahead if you want, and devote all sorts of time to what is supposed to motivate people to do their best! I want my students to play <u>for</u> <u>the</u> <u>love</u> <u>of</u> <u>music</u>, not for a chance to beat their neighbor! Oh, I suppose you can use the same arguments that justify other sorts of tests, but, in my estimation, major motivation should come from within, as it should in all art, and for that matter, <u>all</u> of life!

With this approach you can place everyone where they can do the most good. In this regard I still cherish the memory of one of my female students, bless her heart! Even as a senior she served admirably as a 3rd cornet player where she could enhance the section (and she is still one of our most appreciative alumni)! As you might suspect, in a tryout situation a senior, not capable of rising to the top, could easily be inclined to quit the ensemble rather than feel shamed by playing lower parts…even though one of the many problems of fine balance is lack of strength in inner voices!

"Challenges!" Oh, how I detest that word when referring to chair position! One of the kinds of challenge I am interested in is the challenge to play solos! Get a collection book and play everything in it! Or, organize small ensembles! Do an outstanding job of helping with fund-raising! There are some <u>real</u> challenges for you!

OLDER BEGINNERS!

I think, no matter how big a school, if at all possible, some attention should be given to older beginners. What a pity to prohibit music study to students just because they didn't have the opportunity to start in fifth grade! Since I taught in smaller "B" and "C" schools, we benefited by training students no matter at what age level! Right now I want to mention one fine girl who started French horn in the summer <u>after</u> her junior year! Do you know she became one of our most loyal students, bought her own instrument, and, in her church, after graduation she was instrumental in beginning an orchestra which is, still today, a fine organization! Older beginners learn quickly and are very helpful in filling possible gaps in your instrumentation by using school instruments.

CONDUCTING! Oh! Wow! Is THIS ever a "fun" topic! All that follows is only <u>my</u> opinion so, of course, you are expected to do as you please with the information!

One hand with a baton; use <u>it</u> to define the beats! Don't use a baton and then conduct with your hand as though the baton were not there! The training I received emphasized seeming to "tap" an imaginary surface just above the level of the music stand. This provides a "point" to each beat and makes the tip of the baton the important focus. This approach allows for a more conservative amount of motion by the hand…and what about that left hand? I hope you won't always use it to "mimic" the other hand except for strong emphasis at times! Be coordinated enough to do <u>other</u> important things with that free hand! Use it to cue, indicate dynamics, make cut-offs, etc.

Oh boy! I just recalled another source of dissatisfaction about the conducting I have often witnessed! Unnecessary "preparatory beats!" True, I can't consider myself the greatest conductor in the world, but I <u>never</u> signaled tempo to a group in <u>any</u> way other than with the <u>speed</u> and <u>style</u> of <u>one</u> preparatory beat! How often I have seen a director count out four and even eight beats and then get a lousy attack anyway! (Sometimes the director even proceeds with a tempo different from the one he indicated!)

I feel very comfortable using a sub-divided beat when appropriate. This is something I have a habit of monitoring whenever I have occasion to watch a conductor. It seems so practical at times but I don't really see anyone use it. For example: the final phrases of the Star Spangled Banner. (It is really going to be a challenge to put this into words!)
  "Oh, say does that Star Spangled Ba-n-ner-er ye-et way-ave?"
   1–an -2–an-3-an-1-an-2

Cut-off of "two" at the same time becomes the preparatory beat for count "three" pick-up to next phrase. This is also an example of what I prefer for the last two phrases…all the while allowing for a very controlled ritard! So! Rather than the usual ill-defined beats I observe, and even less desirable "pokes in the air" to cue the various notes in the phrase endings, I recommend the orderly, practical use of the sub-divided beat.

Let's use posture to telegraph style! A brisk march should find you very erect, feet together in an almost military pose. A relaxed posture would be appropriate for something that expresses more intense feeling. Try to avoid a monotonous movement of the body. Enjoy the possibility of helping to make a visual interpretation of the music! And, cue like mad, not just to aid performer's entrances, but also to direct the attention of your audience to the sections of importance at the moment. This provides a welcome bit of variety for everyone.

A serious word here to lady conductors…and they are welcome, and more and more in evidence as I write this. For goodness sake, be careful in your selection of clothes for the occasion! Men really do not have the problems to the degree you face. Your choices <u>can</u> be distracting! I have a picture in mind of looking at a charming young lady…with a big conspicuous run in the back of her stocking! How do you discipline yourself not to be distracted by that? Not only by what you see, but also, in addition, by visions of how she will feel if she finds out! Something too sheer, and you may reveal more than you intended. And…those movements you might make! I have seen feet too far apart and "pumping" motions that would have embarrassed Elvis!

CONCERT COMMENTS!

Can't we take a lesson from TV? A purposeful introduction to the selections we perform cannot be all that bad. If there is nothing notable (pun intended) about a composition, perhaps it isn't worth presenting! It is beneficial to have an audience have their attention focused on various aspects of that which they are about to hear. Gone are the days when it is considered an insult to the audience's intelligence if you provide information they probably have no way to access except by your enlightenment. And…please…let your comments be concise and delivered without reading! (I always had a standing joke that I must go home and "prepare my spontaneous remarks!") I once had occasion to recommend that a particular director should consider comments to his audience and, do you know, he actually <u>read</u>, "I wish you a Merry Christmas!"

All of this leads me to another item you can learn from TV; the use of the microphone! How is it that we can observe all these singers holding that "mic" close to their teeth, and yet, those who don't know any better, distance themselves from it so far that there is no way to have an acceptable sound of "presence" or volume unless the amplifier is turned up so high that you get that terrible "feedback" or distortion? Also, as you speak you should listen to yourself to monitor the sound you are making so you can judge your quality and adjust your distance accordingly. (Much as a musician must listen to himself as he plays.)

MUSIC BOOSTERS!

I hope you realize that some of the parents of your students will be <u>eager</u> to assist you in developing a real active music program. LET THEM! As I write this I am visualizing a personal music program close to my heart and here are some of the things the parents contribute:

1. Sponsor fund-raising: Plan, advertise; attend to all aspects!
2. Issue uniforms: Measure for new, distribute and collect.
3. Chaperone: Everything from concerts to festivals and trips.
4. Set-up crews: Adult responsibility for moving equipment.
5. Program ads: Solicit community businesses and professionals.
6. Archives: Photos, trophy cases, and even web site!
7. Activism: Very diplomatic dealing with administrators.
8. Transportation: All sorts of opportunity.
9. Coaching: Some are capable of conducting sectionals at camp.
10. Camp councilors.
11. Color guard instructors: and,
12. Help with music library; always a big chore!

Caution! Be willing to allow Boosters the freedom to run their own organization! Do not undermine their opportunity to serve in a responsible manner, independent of you. Be there just to assist but not to govern although you will always have to reserve the right to be personally responsible for all areas that belong exclusively to the director – choosing music, grading, etc.

CLASS DISMISSAL!

The rehearsal is ended! Everyone is more relaxed! Almost everyone is in a hurry! What an excuse for pandemonium! What a reason for some of the disorder in the room that remains once the class has left!

This might be a "hangover" from days in the military, but even though you have wonderfully disciplined students in your organization, and even though their behavior is exemplary when playing or marching in public, I would like to suggest that, especially with the younger bands, upon the conclusion of the rehearsal they should properly "stow" their equipment and folios and then stand behind their chairs until you conduct a brief "inspection!" Is everything now in order? Class dismissed!

CHAPTER EIGHT: MARCHING BAND!

Ugh! A necessary evil? That is one way to look at it, especially if you are a fine musician with your main interest being superb performance of fine musical literature, and especially if your musicians are personally very serious about playing their principal instrument proficiently! But, we are teachers, and we conduct ensembles, and in schools and communities we have many other obligations, and don't you forget it!

Yes! We must serve our schools and the public. Deservedly so! And we should be very willing to use our ensembles in every way that can be justified. For example:

1. Band shows at athletic events;
2. Parades of many sorts, even though some of the events interfere with our preparations for concerts and even though some of the events expose us to inclement weather. (I think of Santa Claus!)
3. Civic affairs and patriotic functions, especially Memorial Day, when many band members want to be somewhere else!
4. Community benefit performances.

Football shows; here we have a definite decision to make! Do we use what may now be considered by some to be "obsolete"...the shows made of formations and "tailor made" with new material each performance? Or, do we use what has been called "Corps Style," which is so intricate that it cannot possibly be changed every performance and, in fact, may require preparation way in advance of the marching season, even including a special pre-school camp? Oh, the "midnight oil" I burned, planning a different show for each game!* Drills, dance steps, formations and coordinated scripts and props and even, sometimes, lighting! (The latter in this day and age probably would no longer be permitted, I suppose.) Oh, the "agony" of having to change the plans when weather did not allow for adequate preparation of the entire scenario! All rehearsing was done during class time, which really demanded very efficient use of every minute.

This approach did have the advantage of providing timely entertainment with plenty of variety from show to show and I will admit there was a time when I considered that this was the only "fair" way to treat the spectators. Much of our drilling was based on the four-man squad, "eight-to-the-yard-line," with "high-stepping!" This provided an efficient method of planning and assigning field positions for entrances, formations, etc. Bill Moffitt, a band director at Michigan State in the early

---

*   Lucky you if you can take advantage of computer programs presently available for planning your shows!

sixties, expanded this technique into a very popular system called "Patterns in Motion." As you might expect, even though the system was very beneficial in show planning, there was an understandable need for more variety than could be attained by consistent use of it. Contrary to presentations I witness today, by use of this "squad" approach my band drilled its way onto the field, from the sidelines, striking up school songs only <u>seconds</u> after the horn sounded for half-time. I still consider this effective as opposed to the time-consuming entrances I have seen in recent years. (I am a bit "suspicious" of a desire to "pad" the program by using precious minutes just to enter the field!)

As an example of a show I was proud to present, in spite of all the planning required, I would like to site one where we did a "This is Your Life" in honor of an esteemed coach…a complete surprise because he, in his enthusiastic, helpful manner, even motivated his classes to help with the fund-raising for the event, not knowing that <u>he</u> was to be the honored guest! Imagine his surprise when we had him called to the field, ushered to a convertible, greeted on the P.A. by recorded voices of former athletes who then walked out to greet him personally, and for a final touch, presented him with camera, projector and screen; gifts which introduced him to the hobby of photography that he pursued for the rest of his life! For a portion of Homecoming shows we erected a 30' movie screen and showed slides of the previous year's Queens and Class floats. Oh, how the kids reacted when they saw what they had done the previous year! (In the appendix we will diagram our method of making the screen, but as stated above, turning out the field lights might not be feasible anymore.)

Now, for the second option of marching performance: "Corps Style," with its smooth, "heel-to-toe" characteristic gliding steps! Hey! I used to think it was so unjust…to subject an audience to the same show each week! But…I have been converted! Remember my remark about burning the " midnight oil?" Wow, you don't <u>do</u> that with this method…instead you do all the planning months in advance…rehearse it early in the season! (Some schools even start before school dismisses in spring.) The crowd seems to enjoy watching the improvements and additions from week to week, especially as they realize you are getting ready for competition against schools from other cities. Band members get the added incentive of traveling to other sites, and, with the prevailing mood being that everyone likes to compete for ratings, you have motivation to attain high performance quality, fund-raising, parental involvement and lots of recognition!

If you run a successful program, the rewards are really special! The spirit generated in the community goes way beyond that which you attain with four or five football shows per year. You <u>do</u> need lots of fund-raising for this approach, however, and <u>lots</u> of cooperation, and <u>lots</u> of evening rehearsal to bring together elements that are not always available during class time. During evening rehearsals you <u>do</u> have a chance to include students who may have had schedule conflicts, or extra students who serve as flag corps, etc. All things considered, if you have the ambition and the cooperation, Corps Style has a lot to recommend it!

Whatever course you follow, plan to really capitalize on the opportunity to give worthwhile exposure to your music program! As directors, we owe a lot to the people, at all levels, which support our endeavor. You may not have a great desire to develop a marching band, but especially those parents who pay the bills, should be provided more than a "Christmas" and a "Spring Concert" to enjoy!

Speaking of having extra performances, how about the "Blast from the Past!" This is a fine conclusion to a marching season! Indoors…no rain…no freezing temps'…just a fine opportunity to play all those songs under ideal conditions! We start with a "raucous" entry down the aisles with full percussion…up on the stage we go…up onto the risers we have been touting in this treatise…a few whistles and a roll introduces "The Star Spangled Banner!" Gee, I'm getting' emotional just thinking about it!

Drum Major and majorettes and flags all get their chance to shine, too! Then, after playing about half of the seasons' tunes…time out, and we let the band rest while we present a slide show of Homecoming! (Does that ever go over great at an assembly program, especially when the kids get another glimpse of the floats they worked so hard to construct!) Wait a moment we're not done yet…we show some film highlights of the football team with the coach doing the narrating! And…now, we finish with the <u>rest</u> of the show tunes and end with all the school songs! We really made an entertaining night of it! Put that marching music AWAY! Oops! Forgot the Christmas Parade!

Here is a view of the Westood Heights, Hamady Band, Flint, Michigan, in position for the "1974 Blast from the Past!" Note the benefit from having risers that are in 1-foot increments.

We may as well also show the use of risers for the "Stage Band" to be discussed in the next chapter.

CHAPTER NINE: MORE ENSEMBLES!

JAZZ BAND!

Gone are the days when formal music departments frowned upon students being involved in Stage Bands or Jazz Bands. (Reminds me of the time in college, as a beginning clarinet student, I was admonished by the head of the department for playing a "sub-tone" version of "I'm Confessin' That I Love You!") Jazz Bands have become an attractive addition to the functions of a really active music department.

The instrumentation required induces students to add to their musical experiences in many ways: Play secondary instruments, read advanced rhythms, use many new articulations, become featured soloists, and, especially to improvise. (There are some fine materials available to help, develop this skill. See "bibliography.")

There is also the opportunity to enter competition in festivals organized by State Musical organizations. Jazz Band can be a fine addition to concert programs and, as you might expect, the literature available is very adaptable for many occasions and is very well received by young and old alike.

It is often desirable to include a "vocalist" with these groups. Allow me to register one of my pet "peeves!" The use of a "mic!" Why, oh why, can't people learn by observation! Singers on TV always have it very close to the lips. There is no better way to get the feeling of "presence!" Turning up the amp to enhance the volume just causes all sorts of problems, yet, you will so often notice ineffective use of the microphone…and by public speakers, too!

Since I have just alluded to "learning by observation," I would like to recommend something I do, with my propensity for "picking people's brains!" That is, I try to learn everything I can by watching TV performers, especially orchestras, where I can observe bowing techniques of the strings, embouchures, fingering and instrument positions of the winds, and even the antics of the percussion section. I shall go a step further…use the Internet. There is nary a topic, that you might request, that will not be addressed; sometimes to lengthy degrees!

PEP BAND

This, like marching band can be a big inconvenience when trying to do serious work with the major ensembles in a music department. However, as with marching band, you may as well capitalize on the extra exposure your group will experience. Then, too, it is a fine opportunity for the students to play secondary instruments, play lots of "lighter" music, (get into ball games free), gets lots of repetition of "school songs," include younger musicians even though they are not yet in senior bands, and, if you are really ambitious, to set-up quasi-jazz band and present featured vocals that appeal so much to the younger crowd. And, we don't dare forget the primary function of the pep band; <u>support the team and cheerleaders</u>!

Do expect a real 'headache' when it comes to doing all the library work to provide the folios for all the music needed for a group like pep band! It can be rather hectic trying to distribute parts to loosely formed organizations like this and you will lose music if you are not really careful.

PIT BAND/ORCHESTRA

This gives me the opportunity to introduce a conviction of mine. "<u>A "musical" can be one of the most rewarding events a music department can present!</u>"

When you combine drama, voices, lighting, props, scenery and then a "Pit Band," you can provide a wholesome experience for many individuals and for many departments of the school plus quality entertainment for a host of citizens…taxpayers in the community!

In the early sixties, we didn't have much exposure to musicals in the schools, and we started very gingerly with relatively easy but very entertaining presentations. Before long we graduated to full-fledged "Broadway Musicals!" Sure, the royalties were a problem and the pit band/orchestra had demanding parts in ranges and key signatures that were guaranteed to expand your musical horizons (often requiring adult participation, which was not all bad) but the rewards were so satisfying to all involved, and so memorable! I will conclude by reinforcing the notion…musicals are one of the finest contributions we can present with all these skills we have developed. It is a big challenge to be sure and, unfortunately the pit band/orchestra has a limited size, but, if possible, don't miss the opportunity!

SOLO & ENSEMBLE!

Really beneficial, but, so difficult to schedule! It is logical to have students perform as members of small ensembles. There are so many possible combinations to consider and so many different opportunities to use these small performing groups, but, wow; how to efficiently select the appropriate music for each type of ensemble at each level of difficulty? Then there is the additional problem of finding capable accompanists for soloists, not to mention how to schedule rehearsal time! Let's admit that it is an almost impossible task to do all that would be desirable in the area of solo and ensemble training and performance in spite of the fact that it is something every serious student should have a chance to experience! A library that contains all that could be needed is difficult to acquire and maintain. Just the filing system alone is a challenge! There is so much reason to recommend it! One item, in addition to local performances, is the favorable impression this sort of activity makes when included in a college entrance résumé. One has to hope that the students themselves will accept the responsibility to become involved in this worthwhile endeavor. Fortunately, private instruction can also foster participation.

VOCAL MUSIC!

You may have noticed several references to vocal music thus far; evidence of the respect I think this facet of the musical world deserves! In fact, perhaps the majority of aspiring band directors will, at some stage in their careers, be called upon to devote some attention to singing! It may be just a vocal soloist included in some feature in one of your concerts. Even more possible, especially in a smaller school situation, an instrumental teacher may also be scheduled to direct a choir. Face it! You might consider this so undesirable as to react unfavorably to the responsibility, however, in my opinion; anything "vocal" is even more fundamental in the human experience, than is "instrumental!" After all, the voice is an important part of us…an instrument isn't!

In a practical school situation, use of vocal performance can range from everyone singing school songs to participation in talent shows, musicals, benefits and ceremonies like graduation. True, many times the rehearsals are "early bird," after school or in the evening, but, with the advent of "seven period days," choir is more frequently a part of the school day!

My experience, in "Class B" schools, included some grade vocal plus choirs before school, during school hours, or during an "activity period." Participation is somewhat limited during school hours. Understandable, especially if you want that "student accompanist" who may already have a rather full schedule. (Thankfully, I never directed a choir that didn't have a capable student accompanist!) When all students are available, I did have as many as 140 in the choir! (Once, after hearing the fellows singing in the locker room, I called them the "locker room canaries," and had 40 boys join our group!)

Allow me to register my disgust with the practice of having choirs sing along with recorded accompaniment! My favorite passion is to aim for "a cappella" performance. I don't really like the sound of a piano with voices, however, there *is* much suitable music where piano is absolutely essential…and is always needed in rehearsal to help locate pitches for each voice.

I would like to suggest a few simple techniques to give you the confidence to face potential "singers!" If you ask students to "hum," when they open their mouth to sing "mah, may, mee, mo, moo," good vocal tone should be emitted if they are humming correctly; otherwise the lips move…and nothing else happens! Two more items: first, assume a smile, with teeth showing, and, pucker the lips forward (as though beginning to say, "shout"). With these few "aides," it is almost impossible to have faulty tone production! Use a full breath, sustain tone on vowels, and then, save consonants for cut-offs! Now, you are ready to use, what you just learned, to enjoy directing a choir!

CHAPTER TEN: PRIVATE INSTRUCTION!

Don't miss this valuable opportunity, no matter how busy you think you are!

Here are some reasons why:

1. Train older students who missed band in the early grades.
2. Fill needed instrumentation in your performing ensembles.
3. "One on one" training cannot be surpassed.
4. Opportunity to monitor the quality of your teaching.
5. Gain insight regarding variety of problems students encounter.
6. Chance to evaluate "new" approaches to problem solving.
7. Assign materials not normally used in large ensembles.
8. Prepare students for competition and auditions.
9. Prepare "serious" students who may want to follow in your footsteps.
10. Earn extra cash! (A big help to an "entry level" teacher especially since the salary was $3,200 for a Master's Degree in 1949…my first year.)

As you may imagine, the "atmosphere" is so completely different when you teach privately as opposed to the conditions you face during the school day, especially when you normally teach large groups. In this private situation you will be able to give much help to those who need it, and you can also give advanced training to those who are anxious to have it!

Even meeting the parents before or after a session has additional value because of all sorts of "feedback" you will experience. You also have the opportunity to discuss the student's progress and make useful suggestions

I cannot help but reemphasize the value of working under such ideal conditions; sharing your knowledge with a student who is usually highly motivated. It can be an extremely beneficial situation for both of you! A word of caution, however! Every minute is costing money; so don't waste precious time. I recall one student whose teacher actually spent part of his lesson time on the telephone! You want your lessons to be a real bargain! Even though I usually "stretch" their lesson time, I want to include emphasis on (1) technique, (2) new material, (3) solos and (4) sight-reading. This can be difficult to accomplish as students so often request help with music for their school or church, etc.

Be advised, you need to consider the extra responsibilities you assume when you offer private instruction…as opposed to what was expected in the classroom! Now you are faced with what must be considered a business! You need to maintain a fee structure with records for income tax purposes. In addition, you will have to commit to scheduling and securing appropriate materials for both study and performance! Of course, providing a "recital" is a worthwhile addition for your students.

Let's "gossip" a bit here! Realize, as of this writing, January 2, 2012, I have been teaching privately for over 62 years, in addition to my public school work…and I love it! I have to wonder why more retired teachers don't get involved? The friendships with my students (ages 8 – 65…violins, trumpets, French horn, trombone, flute and sax) are precious and I can hardly wait to see them from week to week! Oh, how I recommend private teaching! Something I just recently noted; you only get to interact with nice people, both students and family! Probably, because it is a rather select group…students who are anxious to improve, and family that is sincere about doing everything they can for their loved ones! What a bargain!

Now, back to the subject! When you have need to prepare students for auditions and public performance, whether you like it or not, your reputation is on the line! I may have called your attention to this previously, but it bears repeating…plan to pay attention, not only to the quality of performance, but also, stage presence! At recitals, or any presentation, for that matter, the appearance matters, too! I don't know about your standards, but I <u>can</u> tolerate a "flub" or two, but to see poor posture, poor bowing technique, faulty hand positions, etc. is intolerable!

At times I take pictures to show students how they look…hiding behind a music stand, especially violin, where it is preferable for the audience to get a "side view" of hands and bowing…or, the trumpeter with head bowed and horn even lower!

In preparation for performances have your students consider this; **"knowing you have adequately prepared yourself, leads to the confidence needed to conquer possible stage-fright!"** (If mouth is dry, lightly bite the tip of your tongue. Also, for relaxation, refer to the breathing exercises mentioned earlier in this text.)

Need I mention the pride and joy I feel when my students are asked to demonstrate their skills or when they succeed with the many opportunities that become available to them? Am I being too "vain" when I share with you the fact that it pleases me no end, when these same students "keep coming back for more!"

CHAPTER ELEVEN: MUSIC APPRECIATION!

Hey! This is MY book and I'm going to include what I want, and that means I am now going to get rather personal and mention one of my favorite things…MUSIC APPRECIATION!

If <u>you</u> taught a class…and fifty years later former students at class reunions felt motivated to let you know how much benefit they derived from <u>your</u> M.A. classes, you might <u>also</u> want to discuss this topic!

I'm not referring to Junior High classes either! Let me elucidate!

    Full year; full-credit classes for <u>juniors</u> and <u>seniors</u>.
    Eligibility: No restrictions!
    High scholarship or low!
    Previous musical training or none!
    Small school or large school: small school to fill your schedule; large school because you have assistants.

Allow me to describe the classes. We didn't care if class size was more than fifty, and the background of the participants was of no consequence. One of the first revelations that set the tone for the rest of the course was my drawing a tiny little circle in the corner of the blackboard and informing the class that, <u>that</u> was to represent the school band, and…the <u>rest</u> of the board represented the rest of the field of music! So much for the advantage band members would have over the rest of the class!

Each student needed to enter information in a notebook with sections devoted to:

    <u>Instruments</u>: We spent "hands on" time with every standard band and orchestra instrument, an immediate "hit" with students who had never blown a horn before, or bowed a violin, etc. Also considered was the construction of stringed instruments, immediately providing interesting information and experience for even those who had lots of previous experience with other instruments! Sure, we grouped them in families and, we used Benjamin Britten's *Guide to the Orchestra* to get everyone able to identify all of the instruments by sound!

    <u>Terminology</u>: How helpful it was to have students feel comfortable pronouncing words like "cello" or "Beethoven." By the frequent use of terms, no matter what language, confidence was established and pride was instilled which enabled classmates to be at ease and also to give them an early feeling of accomplishment.

Repertoire: A list of compositions we included in our "journey" through periods, styles, forms and composers.

Form: Examples and familiarity with each of the main forms of music.

Opera: During the course of the year, extensive listening to: *La Boheme*, *Carmen*, *La Perichole*, *Carmen Jones*, *Amahl and the Night Visitors*, and *Hansel and Gretel*. (Each of these was thoroughly tested over several days including complete written synopsis of each act and, unique testing wherein the story had to be written, synchronized with the clock while the music played!) Field trips to operas in Detroit were part of each year.

Music Theory: Simple introduction to the keyboard and chord structure with emphasis on Triads and some Progressions.

History: A bit of time devoted to the characteristics of the various periods and the composers who represented them.

Pipe Organ: A fairly thorough investigation of the "innards" of the traditional organ as well as study about the specifications of the console itself. One memorable field trip found us "inside" the organ in Hill Auditorium, Ann Arbor!

Dancing the Waltz: The inevitable request for some "popular" music (they had to promise to actually listen to it) always led to the opportunity to have everyone learn "steps" to the organized classical dance as opposed to the "freelance" maneuvering at the contemporary discothèque. (Each student had to demonstrate various steps with a partner.)

These topics were not covered as "Units," rather there was a rather simultaneous presentation of various facets that allowed for considerable variety from day to day. Items were to be entered under various headings as the experiences accumulated. (A real problem for me was the checking of each notebook every marking period, but it was worth the effort!)

Once, while studying the Verdi *Requiem*, there was a performance on my little TV on a Sunday afternoon. What flexibility! We met at school to enjoy it…and this was the year I allowed students to bring "lawn chairs" to class so they could listen in comfort!

Annual field trips to hear Handel's *Messiah* were a fine opportunity for fellowship. A nice rapport develops between teacher and student during such events.

We always presented Copland's *Appalachian Spring*, piano concertos by Grieg and Tschaikowsky, symphonies by Mozart, Bizet, Beethoven, Tschaikowsky and Dvorak, suites by Grieg and Grofe, and violin concertos by Mendlessohn and Tschaikowsky.

I did not have as much sympathy for contemporary music as perhaps I should have had, and, somehow, as I write this, I wonder why I didn't include more Bach, Wagner and Brahms? However, these composers were presented, but only with examples of some of their lesser works. Let's face it! It takes more than a year to experience all the goodness of music!
The most important concept we emphasized was that of the value of "familiarity" to the appreciation of music. True, the very advanced listener can find enjoyment in unfamiliar music, but for the most part a lot of our appreciation depends on being familiar with the work. (This is exactly what "disc

jockeys" do for "pop" tunes!) I really like the illustration that calls attention to the fact that, on a journey; the farmer will notice the crops and fields, the businessman will be aware of the billboards, the contractor will observe the new houses, etc. The more interests you, as an individual posses, the more interesting the trip! So it is with music appreciation; the more facets of music with which you are familiar, the more intense your enjoyment will be. Our task then, is to provide the opportunity for students to be exposed to as many musical elements as possible.

I want to close this chapter by calling your attention even more to the "feed back" I have experienced as a result of these classes. Sure, band members have often let me realize their pride and satisfaction with our efforts…but, with obviously good reason, my Music Appreciation students are demonstrating that <u>they</u> received something precious that has <u>even</u> <u>more</u> continuing value! I was jealous of several, who entered the armed forces, and then <u>went</u> <u>to</u> <u>operas</u> <u>in</u> <u>Europe</u>; <u>my</u> enjoyment, however pleasant, limited to houses in New York and Detroit!

One memorable event I would like to share! Remember we offered class to all levels of scholarship? Well, this young man got in trouble with the law and was given the alternative of going to jail or entering the service and, before he left for the Army, he came to my room and asked, once again, to hear the opera, "*Carmen*"!

CONCLUSION!

Well, if you have managed to get this far into this treatise, you just may have discovered some "Aides" that you will be able to utilize, and <u>that</u> would make me proud as you might expect!

Incidentally, while it is not my intent to delve into the categories of basic instrument repair, instrument purchase, uniform purchase, and music acquisition, I feel that a prospective teacher should be forewarned of these additional responsibilities. Further, as if we haven't already given one enough to consider, and somewhat "off the subject," I heartily recommend the present trend of providing an annual trip for your organization. So beneficial!

You have seen that we use an awful lot of exclamation marks in this treatise! Why! Because there are an awful lot of things to emphasize!!! I feel, all too many items seem to be neglected in this task of teaching music!

In retrospect, and with the realization that many are the changes since I earned my degrees, allow me to report that, even with a University that prided itself in all things educational, there were, what I consider, some unfortunate omissions in important facets of teacher-training:

1. Recommendations for fund-raising methods.
2. Show planning; (now, at least, easier with computer programming).
3. Uniform purchase; care and issue.
4. Music library organization for all levels of ability and a myriad of ensembles.
5. Use of news media; and also, now, e-mail, Face book, etc.
6. Instrument repair; at least for predictable, minor problems.
7. Program design and printing.
8. Transportation considerations.
9. Recording techniques.
10. Private tutoring.
11. Band Camp organization and planning. So beneficial, but actually so challenging and demanding!
12. And on and on! One might use the excuse, that, there is <u>too</u> much to do, BUT the successful director will find a way!!!

I'd rather not end all of this section with anything like a "sour note," but my conscience won't allow me to neglect to suggest a bit of caution here. One of my daughter's Detroit Opera Orchestra friends had a son who contemplated being a band director. Unfortunately, when he read the copy of "Heff's Band Aides," he changed his mind! All of which causes me to emphasize the following for the potential reader:

The human animal can become accustomed to anything!
Dostoyevsky (I think!)

Finally, I am aware that it would be impossible to expect total agreement with all of the notions presented here, so, if it is your pleasure, why not avail yourself of the opportunity to discuss my offerings! E-mail address: heff@fmuth.com

"Prepare for the future; enjoy the present; cherish the past!"

Heffelfinger

Bibliography

Fussell, Raymond C. Exercises for Ensemble Drill Miami, Fl. 33014
  CPP/BELWIN, INC. 1967

Hanson, Fay Brass Playing New York, N.Y.
  Carl Fischer, Inc. 1968

Hindsley, Mark H. Wind Instrument Guides Hammond, La.
  From "Tuning the School Band" Ralph R. Pottle 1960

Moffit, Bill Patterns In Motion Winona, Minn.
  Hal Leonard Music Inc. 1965

Rhodes, Ruth Single Reed Adjustment Chicago, IL.
  Vandercook College of Music 2003

Smith, Leonard B. Treasury of Scales for Band Mellville, N.Y.
  Belwin Mills Publishing Corp. 1961

Sorenson & Pearson Jazz Ensemble Method San Diego, CA
  Neil A. Kjos Music Company 1998

Yaus, Grover C. & Roy M. Miller 150 Original Exercises
  Rockville Centre, L.I., New York BELWIN, INC. 1944

Yaus, Grover C. 101 Rhythmic Rest Patterns
  Rockville Centre, L.I., N.Y. BELWIN, INC. 1953

Appendix A – Risers

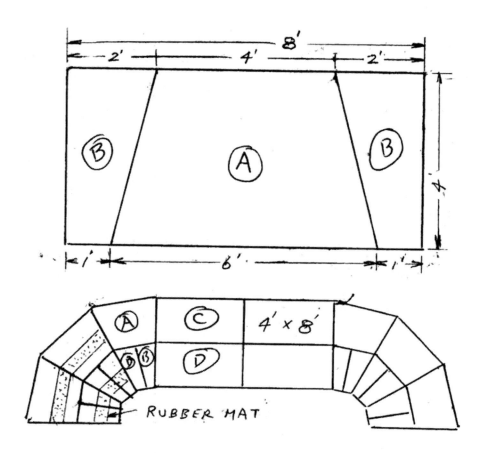

Plans

Needed for set-up depicted above:

6 – Riser "A" (4' x 6' – 2' high)
6 — Riser "B" (2' x 4' – 1' high)
2 — Riser "C" (4' x 8' — 2' high)
2 — Riser "D" (4' x 8' — 1' high)

Recommend use of good ¾ inch plywood for all surfaces with a 1' rubber matt as indicated. If possible use 5/4 lumber for the rails and 2x4 stock for the posts, plowed to a depth of about 7/16-inch for substantial positioning and strength of all joints. Black paint for the frames and floor sealer for the plywood is appropriate. Screws and glue should be used for all fastening.

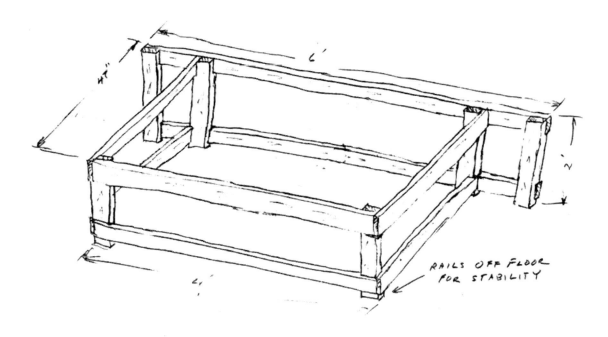

Use this type of construction for all frames, altered for the 4'x8' sections (with the addition of an extra brace in the center of the large frames).

Also, notice how the cut of the 4x8 sheets allow for the smaller "B" segments to be formed. These risers will be 1' high and will need a center frame to support the joint of the plywood when you connect the two segments.

The depth of the frames is purposely 47" to allow for a one-inch nosing (overhang) of the flooring on the front of each frame. Install a 1"x1" chair-rail at the back of 2' risers.

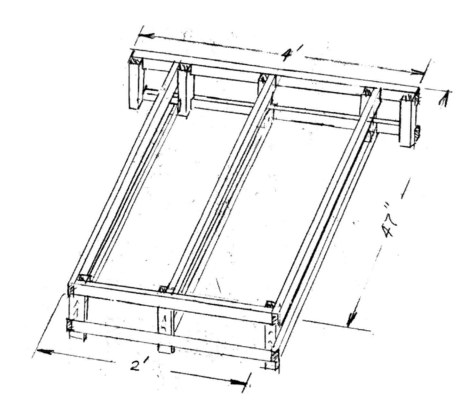

The above illustrations are corner posts (L) and (R). You will need two of each for each riser, 2-foot lengths for the 8-2' high risers in the set-up, 1-foot lengths for the 8 lower risers. Notice that there are "pockets" or "insets" where the rails are fastened. (Glued and screwed.)

The 4'x8' risers will also need a pair of these posts to reinforce the center of each section.

In addition, below is an illustration of the 2-foot posts that are used on the outside corners of the back of the 4'x6' risers.

Appendix B – A-Frame

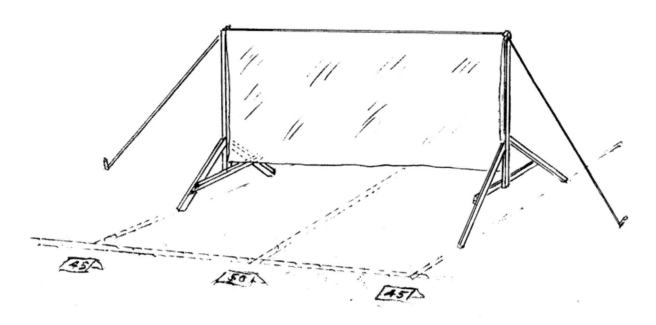

Here it is! The "A" frame we promised! If you have the courage, this is what can be done! Notice on the diagram we have drawn "stakes" on the end of the ropes. This was done only because we were not capable of drawing the majorettes, which were the ones who usually handled this project! Let us describe the way this 30-foot screen (even "cheese cloth" will do) can be erected by six student aides in less than a minute!

Off to the side, with everything fastened as you see on the diagram; (1) lay one frame on top of the other, (2) six aides run out with the frames and, (3) place the foot of the bottom frame on the 45-yard line, (4) three aides stay with bottom frame while other three aides lift top frame and run with it to the opposite 45-yard line and, (5) using the top line, pull the frames to the standing position till it looks like the illustration!

At times we showed film and slides, which it might be noted show even more vividly on the back side of the thin screen (image reversed, of course) because that was direct light whereas, the front side was merely reflected light which is adequate, but not as strong.

Audience thoroughly enjoyed seeing queens and floats from previous year. We imagine there can be other uses of this suggestion. Good luck to all!

Appendix C – French Horn String Replacement

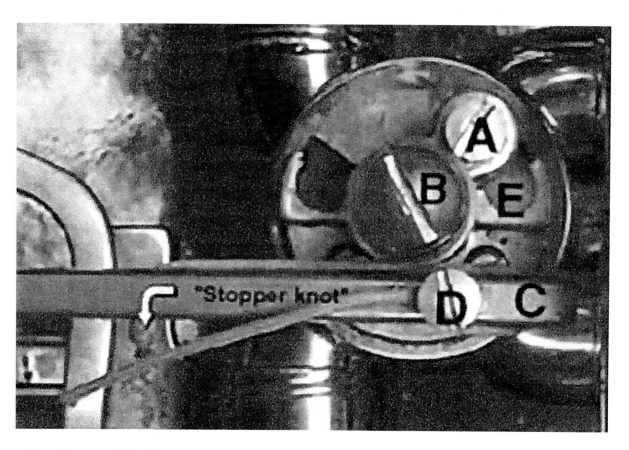

Step 1. Tie figure eight "stopper" knot – thread as shown.
Step 2. Wrap around screw "A" clockwise (Do not tighten screw yet).
Step 3. Wrap around cylinder "B" counter clockwise.
Step 4. Thread through hole "C."
Step 5. Wrap around screw "D" (Do *not* tighten screw yet!).
Step 6. Remove all "slack" in thread.
Step 7. Tighten screw "D."
Step 8. Hold "A" against "limiter" "E."
Step 9. Align "key spatula" with other keys (allow string to slide around screw "A."
Step 10. Tighten screw "A." (And pray!)

Appendix D – Single Reed Adjustment
By Ruth Rhodes, Graduate Dean & Clarinet Instructor, Vandercook College of Music

Purchase a slightly higher reed strength than is normal for you (3 1/2 or 3 3/4); wood can always be taken off. Reeds that are too soft do not have enough heart to produce a full rich sound in all registers. Always view new reeds as unfinished products. Assume that none of them will play right from the box well enough to suit you.

1. Age the reed through storage if possible. Date the box so you know when it was purchased and store in a dry place that has a fairly even temperature.

2. Sand the back of the reed on fine sandpaper and glass until the back is uniformly shiny (don't worry about the tip). The purpose of this step is to flatten the back and correct the warpage, not to thin the reed.

3. Place the reed on the glass side (no sandpaper) and polish the cut portion with reed rush that is slightly flat and softened, until the reed is shiny. Do not press hard enough to remove any wood!

4. Do not try to select a reed by its looks. Reed cane varies too much for this procedure to be trustworthy.

5. After tabling, wet the entire reed until the tip is no longer wavy or warped, and water has been siphoned through to the bottom of the reed.

6. Play test the reed on your clarinet in all registers for about 30 seconds.

7. Lay the reed on a flat surface to dry and go on to the next reed. Follow this procedure 2 times per reed. The play testing time may be extended after the second tabling. Tabling and soaking an entire box of reeds at one time is the most efficient approach for de-warping your reeds.

8. On the final de-warping, adjustments can be made if necessary.

9. Usually the only adjustment necessary is that of balancing the tip.

    a. Check the balance by tonguing forte, accented notes on open G on each side of the apex of the heart.
    b. If the response is the same, the reed is balanced.
    c. If one side is more resistant or "tubby" in sound, use reed rush to shave a few grains of wood from that side of the reed in the area next to the resistance point.

11. I don't advocate clipping the tip of a reed. If the tip is too thin, give the reed to a friend or put it away for very cold weather and go on to the next reed.

12. Whenever unresponsiveness creeps in after playing the reed for several practice sessions, sand the back again and make any necessary minor adjustments.

13. When the reed can no longer be played satisfactorily (the life of an average reed is about 10 hours of playing time), store it; do not throw it away! At a later time under different atmospheric conditions, the reed may play well again.

Appendix E – Snowman

No matter how many times I have used this, it has served as an effective additional event in concert presentations, especially for younger groups. Following is a description of the "gimmick!" Use your own ingenuity to incorporate shop, art and drama to avail yourself of this bit of "fun" at a concert accompanied by either vocal or instrumental versions of "Frosty the Snowman."

Build a bottom for the snowman, large enough to "house" a "secret" accomplice. Include a way to fasten a middle section to the snowman and also build a "head" for the snowman. Use "paper mache" to make a realistic snowman that can be constructed on stage during the playing of the song.

Push the bottom section of the snowman onstage and the have "extras" in outdoor attire complete the "building" of the snowman by adding the remaining sections, finishing with buttons, carrot nose, eyes, and hat, whereupon…what do you know, the snowman starts to move!

Just slight turning, even though you may have seen this done before, still is an eerie sight! You take it from there!

We even added a "scary" moment by having the snowman move precariously close to the front edge of the stage. (Very safe maneuver because the student in the snowman can easily see the stage under his feet.) Add a little snow from a snow machine in the ceiling, and you have an enjoyable contribution to your event!